'This will be an invaluable resource for students, academics and the wider public who want to understand how deep inequalities mark our education system'.
— **Mike Savage**, *Professor of Sociology, London School of Economics and Political Science*

'This ground-breaking book brings a range of critical theories to bear on the global problems posed by our elite universities. Through an original theoretical lens and intensive empirical research, Bhopal and Myers set a critical fire beneath the virtue signalling marketing and positioning of the luxury brands of the worldwide Higher Education sphere'.
— **Professor John Preston**, *University of Essex*

'As this book demonstrates, with devastating clarity and detailed analysis, the truth is that elite universities operate as engines of class and race inequity. Elite universities market themselves as places of privilege and they fulfil an extraordinarily important role in legitimating and reproducing the racist and class structures upon which they feed'.
— **David Gillborn**, *Editor-in-Chief*, Race Ethnicity and Education

ELITE UNIVERSITIES AND THE MAKING OF PRIVILEGE

Providing an extraordinary picture of the inner workings of elite universities, *Elite Universities and the Making of Privilege* draws on current debates on education and inequality and considers the relevance of universities' global brand identities.

Using the work of Bourdieu and critical race theory to explore how identity, experience and family background affects how people navigate the social space of the university, this book is underpinned with empirical research that considers different social, economic and educational contexts. Using interview accounts of graduate students, this book highlights ambiguities in how eliteness works as both a recognisable marker of institutional status and a marker that is rarely quantified or defined.

Combining intellectually rigorous, accessible and controversial chapters, *Elite Universities and the Making of Privilege* is crucial reading for anyone looking to understand how race and class affect those navigating elite universities.

Kalwant Bhopal is Professor of Education and Social Justice and Director of the Centre for Research on Race and Education at the University of Birmingham.

Martin Myers is a sociologist of education in the School of Education at the University of Nottingham.

ELITE UNIVERSITIES AND THE MAKING OF PRIVILEGE

Exploring Race and Class in Global Educational Economies

Kalwant Bhopal and Martin Myers

Routledge
Taylor & Francis Group

LONDON AND NEW YORK

Cover image: © Getty Images

First published 2023
by Routledge
4 Park Square, Milton Park, Abingdon, Oxon OX14 4RN

and by Routledge
605 Third Avenue, New York, NY 10158

Routledge is an imprint of the Taylor & Francis Group, an informa business

British Library Cataloguing-in-Publication Data
A catalogue record for this book is available from the British Library

Library of Congress Cataloging-in-Publication Data
Names: Bhopal, Kalwant, author. | Myers, Martin, 1963– author.
Title: Elite universities and the making of privilege : exploring race
    and class in global educational economies / Kalwant Bhopal,
    Martin Myers.
Description: Abingdon, Oxon ; New York, NY : Routledge, 2023. |
    Includes bibliographical references and index.
Identifiers: LCCN 2022036633 (print) | LCCN 2022036634 (ebook) |
    ISBN 9780367466060 (hardback) | ISBN 9780367466077 (paperback) |
    ISBN 9781003029922 (ebook)
Subjects: LCSH: Universities and colleges—Sociological aspects. |
    Education, Higher—Social aspects. | Graduate students—Attitudes. |
    Elite (Social sciences) | Privilege (Social psychology) | Educational
    equalization.
Classification: LCC LC191.9 .B56 2023 (print) | LCC LC191.9 (ebook) |
    DDC 378—dc23/eng/20221110
LC record available at https://lccn.loc.gov/2022036633
LC ebook record available at https://lccn.loc.gov/2022036634

ISBN: 978-0-367-46606-0 (hbk)
ISBN: 978-0-367-46607-7 (pbk)
ISBN: 978-1-003-02992-2 (ebk)

DOI: 10.4324/9781003029922

Typeset in Bembo
by Apex CoVantage, LLC

MIX
Paper | Supporting responsible forestry
FSC
www.fsc.org   FSC™ C013985

Printed in the United Kingdom
by Henry Ling Limited

For our parents
Swaran Kaur Bhopal and Maureen Myers
with love
Peter Myers and Gian Chand Bhopal
in loving memory

CONTENTS

ABOUT THE AUTHORS

Kalwant Bhopal is Professor of Education and Social Justice and Director of the Centre for Research on Race and Education at the University of Birmingham, UK. She has written extensively on how processes of racism, exclusion and marginalisation operate in predominantly white spaces with a focus on social justice and inclusion.

Martin Myers is a sociologist of education in the School of Education at the University of Nottingham. His work explores patterns of exclusion in different educational settings with a focus on race, racism and social class.

FOREWORD

Virtually every person who has held the office of Prime Minister of the United Kingdom has been a graduate of Oxford or Cambridge. Most were also educated at a limited number of public schools that operate as the access routes to these elite universities. For many, this was just as their parents before them.

This phenomenon is not unique to politics but will be found replicated in most professions and in many commercial circles. The question is whether we should be surprised or shocked by this. Surely this is just the harsh reality of the class system simply replicating itself?

It does however fly in the face of one of the foundational myths of our society that has been used to smokescreen our class system since the late industrial revolution. That we live in an open meritocracy. From the latter years of the nineteenth century the Samuel Smiles ethos has held sway; that a person who works hard enough can pull themselves up by their bootstraps and achieve almost unlimited social advance in their lives.

As it founded the modern educational system the post-war Attlee government embodied this meritocratic commitment with its introduction of access to education free to all. Education was seen as one of and possibly the most important driver of equality in society. The bright-eyed idealism of many of the generation that elected that government aimed and planned for a classless society. All the evidence of the last seven decades has confirmed how resilient and resistant to change the old system of class privilege and entitlement has been. Added to that, how resistant it is to reflecting the cultural diversity of our society.

If we are to uphold the quest for equality, as most still profess we should, then we have to return to the issues of class and race and how these factors still shape our lives. We need to unpick and understand how the individual institutions of our society operate to buttress class and race inequality.

This book makes an important contribution in analysing the role of one of these key institutions – the elite universities. The more we understand and evidence the role they play, the greater the opportunity there is for securing change we need if we are to promote equality effectively.

John McDonnell,
Member of Parliament, United Kingdom

ACKNOWLEDGEMENTS

We are particularly grateful to the respondents who participated in the study – for their generosity and willingness to share their stories with us – without them this book would not have been possible. We would also like to thank the gatekeepers who enabled us to have access to the elite universities.

Kalwant: I would like to thank my colleagues in the College of Social Sciences and the School of Education at the University of Birmingham for their continued support for my work. I would also like to thank the staff and students at Harvard University in the Graduate School of Education where I was a visiting professor when the original ideas for this book were born. I am particularly grateful to David Gillborn, John Preston and Martin Dyke, who always give me the time and space to share my ideas and challenge me to push them forward. Many thanks to my mother Swaran Kaur Bhopal and my siblings for their love and support – especially Jazz, who never allowed me to give up.

Martin: My thanks go out to friends and colleagues at Portsmouth and Nottingham. Despite my innate cynicism, half-full glass and gloomy disposition I enjoy your company enormously. Much love as always to my mother Maureen Myers.

We would both like to thank our children who are now adults and always adept in providing astute critiques of our work. Dylan, Yasmin, Deva and Sachin you make us proud every day.

1

INTRODUCTION

Recognising Elite Universities

This book explores the role of 'elite universities' within the global field of higher education from the unique perspective of graduate students[1] studying in both the United States (US) and the United Kingdom (UK). Whilst there is a body of literature that explores undergraduate experiences of elite universities, postgraduate students have not generally received as much attention. Partly this reflects the liminal spaces they occupy between the more rigidly demarcated roles of academics and undergraduates. That liminal status provides a useful lens; our participants were often able to both reflect on their recent undergraduate experience as the process by which they personally invested more heavily within the academic and university structures of elite universities. They were often better informed about institutional practice and the nature of elite universities than many undergraduates whilst at the same time struggling not necessarily with academic demands but rather their social integration within the ethos of these universities. Many of the students we spoke to were also actively pursuing careers as academics in the future. The increasingly global nature of what constitutes an 'elite student' at an 'elite university' was a significant advantage of interviewing students on both sides of the Atlantic who themselves were often not native to their institutions.

These students have the advantage over undergraduates of having successfully navigated three or more years at university and, taking forward their education at master's or doctoral level, and consequently able to offer a more informed insight into the workings of 'elite universities'. 'Elite' in this context is both an overt descriptor of a number of readily defined institutions whose prominence and status often not only appear unassailable but also signals other more covert messaging about what is conferred within the idea of an 'elite' university. Elite in this second sense is often difficult to pin down not least because it often delineates hierarchies

DOI: 10.4324/9781003029922-1

that whilst not entirely imaginary are in no way cast in stone. The backbone of this book is the interview accounts of graduate students; they readily identify the eliteness of their respective institutions and the personal value they anticipate deriving by their attendance. However, their accounts also highlight ambiguities particularly in how eliteness works as both a recognisable marker of institutional status and a marker, which is never clearly defined. Such ambiguities were reflected in many students' discussions of their university 'brand'; of globally recognisable attributions of status that are difficult to quantify or materially define.

A more troubling ambiguity emerged in students' accounts of differentials in the value they would derive from their attendance at elite universities compared to their peers. These differences in outcomes were not simply the result of different abilities or in the amount of effort and endeavour students applied to their studies. The students we interviewed were all well-motivated, ambitious and, as evidenced in the complex processes they navigated through school and university to be where they were, demonstrably well-qualified. Students from different social, racial and ethnic backgrounds all highlighted the impact race and class had on access to elite universities, their experience of studying at an elite university and their anticipated outcomes. In part this is unsurprising and reflects well-documented patterns of inequality throughout all levels of education; significantly though the experiences of graduate students highlighted ambiguities within their experiences and within the recognition of institutional structures as purveyors of an elite education. Whilst the elite university is an institution associated with enabling forms of privilege; by placing restrictions on how that privilege was accessed by students, it reproduces much of the structure of dominant social, economic and political power. As a means by which mobilities can be fostered it became apparent throughout the research that this was an ambiguous expectation, both in the global sense of students looking towards an elite and mobile future and in the sense of upward social mobilities. Many graduate students gained far less from such mobilities because of their social and ethnic backgrounds. These ambiguities are reflected within the ability of elite universities to be both obviously recognisably elite and yet at the same time as discretely disguising their exclusive and restrictive institutional practice.

The Making of Elite Universities

In England five institutions held university status prior to 1900[2]: The Universities of Oxford and Cambridge can both trace their foundational accounts back to the late twelfth century, over 600 years before the establishment of other institutions in Durham, London and Manchester[3] (Rüegg, 2003). In some part, age has a bearing in terms of status; all five universities are widely recognised as elite universities but the 600 years between Cambridge and Durham seemingly counts for something extra. Oxford and Cambridge are conferred the sobriquet of Ancient Universities; Durham, Manchester and London are not, and all three sit beneath Oxbridge in the *recognition* of status. Such recognisability is a key feature of how elites work; there are shared assumptions by elites and non-elites alike of how such status is validated. The *eliteness* of elite universities can be interpreted as a 'social fact' (Durkheim, 2014), a complex phenomenon constituting a university's status (including perceptions of value associated with its age) that is collectively understood. The broadly held, socially assembled perception of elite universities works to constrain a belief that the University of Oxford, for example, could be understood as anything other than an elite university. Mauss ([1925] 1966) identifies how social facts operate within different dimensions, including economic, legal and religious domains, and that they are equally applicable within political or domestic spheres. By intersecting, perhaps ambiguously, across different domains they are 'phenomena which penetrate every aspect of the concrete social system; they concentrate it and constitute its focus, they are the constitutive elements, the generators and motors of the system' (Goffman, 1998: 67). Goffman goes on to note their significance within sociological accounts, such as those of Anthony Giddens, that understand social systems within processes of globalisation (Giddens, 1984; Goffman, 1998). The recognisability of the *eliteness* of elite universities in this sense goes beyond a descriptive account and represents the unassailability of knowledge about that *eliteness*, that is taken for granted and shapes an understanding of the world, what Bourdieu refers to in his discussion of *doxa* (Bourdieu, 1977; 1984). The social understanding of such phenomenon fall within

> an uncontested acceptance of the daily lifeworld, not simply to establish that it is not universally valid for all perceiving and acting subjects, but also to discover that, when it realizes itself in certain social positions, among the dominated in particular, it represents the most radical form of acceptance of the world, the most absolute form of conservatism.
>
> *(Bourdieu and Wacquant, 1992: 73)*

Clearly the age of universities, including the *ancient* status of Oxford and Cambridge, is not the sole piece of knowledge that produces an understanding of eliteness. For some readers, the reference to Ancient Universities in a purely English geographical context will have raised their hackles. The Ancient Universities are generally understood to comprise not only the two aforementioned English institutions, but also St Andrews, Aberdeen, Glasgow and Edinburgh in Scotland and, arguably, Trinity College, Dublin. This skewing of numbers towards Scotland in particular is a useful factoid for anyone wishing to make claims about the respective educational ethos of the home countries. However, dispensing with nationalistic jingoisms, these five institutions are recognisably elite; but as with Durham, Manchester and London they do not possess the same eliteness as that understood in terms of Oxbridge. Both age and geography have a bearing on the type and recognisability of eliteness of all these institutions.

Looking further afield, distinctions between eliteness feature in most national contexts. In the US age and location are also significant. Mirroring the ancient nomenclature, the Ivy League are also known as the Ancient Eight with Harvard University staking its claim to being the oldest founded in 1636. They also sit in close geographical proximity in Northeastern states. *Ivy League* and *Ancient Eight* both hint at the value imbued in identifiable names and nomenclature. The Ivy League's semantic formula has been readily adopted in a number of different contexts to echo its elite recognisability within publicly funded universities (Public Ivies), regional locations (the Southern Ivies) and elite Historically Black Colleges and Universities (HBCUs) (the Black Ivies). As in the UK, the framing of all these institutions identifies them to be elite universities but still recognises the greater elite standing of the Ivy League itself, and within the Ivy League, of particular institutions. In France the *grandes écoles* are privately run universities imbued with elite status; they also tend to have long histories, most are located in Paris and much like Oxbridge and the Ivy League they have adopted complex admissions processes that ensure their exclusivity. Despite these similarities, the recognition of *grandes écoles* elite status is largely restricted to their national context; globally they do not carry the same elite weight of an Oxford, Cambridge, Harvard or Yale.

History, geography and nationality all count for something in the production of eliteness as a recognisable quality of these institutions. In this sense elite universities are bastions of steadfastness whose reputations outlast even the most tumultuous political change. In 2020 Donald Trump successfully pressured Harvard University to return funding for disadvantaged students during the COVID-19 pandemic (Hartocollis, 2020), the assumption remains however, that the institution will retain its influence throughout and beyond his presidency. One readily recognisable feature of elite universities is their connection to power; directly in terms of politicians and senior government officials, but also indirectly amongst members of the media and other high-profile professions, that share a small number of elite universities as their *alma mater*.

In addition to power, elite universities can be understood in terms of their more readily measurable access to wealth. The very large endowments of the most elite universities exceed the gross domestic product (GDP) of many nation states. Vaccaro (2014) makes the point this is a largely unhelpful comparison bearing in mind the institutional reserves of universities and national economic activity are not the same thing; however, in an effort to provide a scale for the enormous wealth at stake he points out that Harvard University's endowment alone in 2014 compared to International Monetary Fund data 'would settle in between Jordan and Latvia – about smack dab in the middle of the world's economies'. Alternatively the endowment could cover the cost of 'a billion nice lobster dinners' (Vaccaro, 2014). Of the ten individual US universities with the greatest endowments, five are members of the Ivy League (Harvard, Yale, Princeton, Pennsylvania and Columbia), four are private research institutions (Stanford, MIT, Notre Dame and NorthWestern) and only one, the University of Michigan, is a public research university (NACUBO, 2020). Harvard tops the list with an endowment of $40.6 billion in 2020 followed by Yale ($31.2 billion) and Stanford ($28.9 billion). The numbers are eye-watering and far exceed their UK counterparts; in the UK the University of Cambridge accounts revealed a comparatively modest £3.4 billion endowment fund though this is matched by individual colleges separate funds.

'Elite' is a grey area with less clear-cut boundaries in other ways. The lines of demarcation between what constitutes an elite and a non-elite university are not easily drawn. In the UK this might be observed in the delineation of the Russell Group; a self-selecting interest group of 24 leading, research-focused universities including the Universities of Oxford and Cambridge. The Russell Group is not so *gauche* as to publicly label itself as an exclusive club for elite universities but is widely recognised to comprise the best universities in the UK. In 2012, for example when the Department for Education (DfE) first published destination data on student progression into higher education, the number of students progressing to Russell Group institutions were specifically detailed compared to those attending other, less elite universities (DfE, 2012). However, simple membership of the Russell Group does not denote a bar above which eliteness is democratically distributed; some members might be identified as the *better Russell Group universities . . .* and some members might identify themselves as *amongst the best of the Russell Group*. The DfE themselves delineated Oxbridge entrants from 'other Russell Group universities' (DfE, 2012). This is unsurprising. Being part of the 'elite' is a competitive enterprise and beyond being recognised as a member of the exclusive ranks of the Russell Group, there is additional pressure to be identified as a better, more elite member within its own hierarchies. This book explores one particular cohort of individuals seeking entry into that competitive process: postgraduate students in American and British universities.

There is evidence to suggest that students entering elite universities often exhibit a range of characteristics, including access to pre-existing economic, cultural and social capitals, that ensure they 'fit' with the ethos and population of these institutions (Bourdieu, 1977; 1996; Zimdars, 2010). One consequence of this related to the expansion of university's global interests has been the emergence and consolidation of a global middle class with access to greater educational choices based on their mobility and wealth (Ball and Nikita, 2014). Findlay et al. suggest that this transnationalism associated with elite, highly mobile groups fosters influential links between elite schools, universities and an elite globalised job market in which the mobility of students is 'part of a wider set of mobility cultures linked to a person's outlook on their entire life-course' (2012: 122). This reflects the demand of a 'transnational capitalist class' (Sklair, 2000) for universities capable of reproducing the 'political and social advantages' enjoyed by their parents (Findlay et al., 2012: 122). The impact of 'global capital' on international networks and occupations (Maxwell and Aggleton, 2013) suggests that elite education is part of the global market place (Kenway et al., 2013).

Contemporaneously, there is evidence to suggest that some students, in particular those from marginalised backgrounds, do not display the same characteristics associated with membership of an elite university. Consequently they often report feelings of being unable to 'fit in' and navigate the university environment (Jack, 2014; Stuber, 2012) and question their sense of belonging (Ostrove and Long, 2007) and feelings of difference (Stephens et al., 2012; 2014). Working-class students often feel out of place compared to their middle-class peers (Binder et al., 2016) and lack confidence to take advantage of opportunities and resources which will impact on their future social mobility and position in the labour market (Lareau, 2003; Jack, 2016; 2019). Black and minority ethnic students consistently describe feeling 'out of place' in higher education institutions (Bhopal, 2018).

One of the key aims of this book is to understand the processes by which graduate students understood their experiences at elite universities. In particular to unravel why some students appear to fit naturally within the world of elite universities and others feel more ambivalently about their experiences.

The Study

In this section we provide an outline of our methodology. We discuss issues of the sample, access, ethics and data analysis and the use of gatekeepers, and provide demographic details of the students who participated in the study, and the different universities from which they were recruited.

Methods

We conducted a total of 49 interviews with postgraduate students studying at two elite universities in the UK and two in the US. We used a snowball sample to select respondents. Once we selected the universities (based on our definition of whether they were defined as 'elite') we used our personal contacts to recruit respondents to participate in the study. At both the UK and one of the US universities one of us had been invited to deliver keynotes and guest lectures, and during this time we approached students to ask them if they would be interested in participating in the study. Students then recommended others who would be interested in participating. We felt the personal contact made a significant difference to the recruitment of respondents, once respondents knew others who had already participated, they themselves were also willing to participate. At the university in the US where we had no prior contacts, we used our personal networks to recruit students to participate in the study. Our contacts described the research to students in one cohort and asked them if they wanted to participate. If they agreed, our contact sent us their email addresses and contact was made. We are aware of some of the disadvantages of using snowball sampling such as a particular selection bias towards a type of respondent, respondents themselves may ask others who are similar to them and are dependent on the subjective choices of the respondents who were first asked to participate (Van Meter, 1990). Snowball sampling may also introduce bias in which individuals are recruited on the basis of the membership of a network and as such those missing from the network will not be included (Griffiths et al., 1993). Atkinson and Flint however suggest, 'The real promise of snowball sampling lies in its ability to uncover aspects of social experience often hidden from both the researcher's and lay person's view of social life' (2001: 4).

Prior to recruiting students, we asked permission from Heads of Departments and Deans to contact students. We outlined the study, including any risks associated with participating (which were minimal). We also shared the consent form and participant information sheet with them. These were then given to participants before they took part in the study. We were aware that we had to negotiate our relationship with the gatekeepers and stressed the importance of the research in relation to providing an in-depth analysis and understanding of student experiences at elite university, particularly in relation to issues of equity, inclusion and social justice. In some sense, we had to 'manage' our relationship with the gatekeepers and were mindful of their role in enabling us to gain access to respondents (Flick, 1998). However, once access was gained all of the gatekeepers continued their interest in the research, but gave us freedom to conduct the research without influencing the findings in any way. We were able to position ourselves, 'in the field so as to secure the necessary time, space and social relations to be able to carry out the research' (Wolff, 2004: 195).

Our research questions were as follows:

1   *What effect does student's prior educational experiences, identity and family background have on their trajectories to elite universities (e.g. race, socio-economic background and gender)?* We wanted to examine students' *journeys* into elite universities (including school and undergraduate experiences) and how these journeys impacted and affected how students themselves understood their own experiences of studying at an elite university. Were there differences in student's experiences based on their own backgrounds and how did this impact on their experiences?
2   *How do students experience and navigate the space of elite universities and its brand identity?* This was based on examining how students once they were part of an elite university were able to position themselves within the elite as a specific brand, which contributed to their own privilege and that of the university.
3   *How do students understand how their prior experiences contribute to perpetuating a system of privilege?* Here we wanted to explore whether students themselves felt that by attending an elite university they were perpetuating a system of privilege. We also wanted to explore if these experiences differed by race and class.

Analysis

Face-to-face interviews were conducted with 40 respondents and nine interviews were conducted via Skype. A total of 30 interviews were digitally recorded and for all others, handwritten notes were taken as students requested and preferred not to be recorded. All of the interviews were either transcribed or typed up for analysis. Data analysis took place throughout the duration of the project. We understood and approached the analysis as a *process* which enabled us to be reflexive about the findings and theorisation. In this way, we were able to develop new themes and develop our theory during the empirical fieldwork – rather than at the very end. We analysed our interview data through a process of thematic analysis which included the use of qualitative data software (NVivo) and handwritten coding. NVivo was used to aid in the sorting and organising of the dataset and enabled us to work efficiently with developing our coding scheme, facilitating depth and sophistication of our analysis (King, 2004). We used thematic analysis as 'a method for identifying, analysing and reporting patterns within data' (Braun and Clarke, 2006: 76). In this process, we were able to identify patterns across the data set, develop codes and derive meaning from the patterns. We coded and developed themes, defining and naming themes and constantly reviewing them. This process enabled us to go back and forth within the dataset, until we were able to derive meaning from the data (Lorelli et al., 2017). By focusing across the whole range of the data set, we were able to make sense of shared meanings and experiences as they were communicated by our respondents. To increase reliability and validity of the coding, both of us cross-checked each of the themes.

Respondent Details

Our respondents were from a range of different backgrounds. They were studying on a range of different postgraduate courses which included the humanities, social and physical sciences. A total of 45 respondents were studying for a postgraduate degree by research (MPhil/PhD) and four for a postgraduate taught degree (MA/MSc). The ages of respondents varied from 22 to 34, and they were from a range of different ethnicities and socio-economic backgrounds (based on their parents' occupations). A total of 28 respondents were female and 21 were male. The majority of students had attended elite universities for their undergraduate degrees and only five had attended universities that were not considered elite or which did not rank highly in league tables. We were particularly interested in postgraduate student experiences in elite universities due to their transitional status between their graduate status and employment, their greater knowledge and understanding of being at an elite university compared to that of undergraduates, as well as the increased likelihood of the respondents considering employment within academia.

Institution Demographics

Our research focused on elite universities whose global recognisability as such was unquestioned. As discussed earlier there are some clear ambiguities associated with such definitions and delineations of universities eliteness; in particular, within mission groups or affiliations there is competition for status and distinctions between institutions about their eliteness. Such recognisability and the emergence of some elite institutions as overtly higher status materialises in a 'Global Super-League' of elite universities identified by *The Economist* (2005). Despite, or as a consequence, of their very limited numbers, this super-league were cited as being particularly identifiable and framed by their Anglo-American locations and the consistency of their ascendancy (so e.g. ten or even 50 years previously, we would still identify the same cohort). The super-league are drawn almost entirely from the Ivy League, Oxbridge[4] and a small number of other Russell Group universities[5] in the UK. Not only are their collective nomenclatures recognisable, they all have global brand names such as Oxford or Cambridge; the LSE (London School of Economics); Harvard or MIT (Massachusetts Institute of Technology). Super-league universities are defined by their exclusivity including the exclusivity of their student selection processes; their ascendancy of global university rankings measuring excellence in research and teaching; their financial security; their ability to generate income and the domination of their alumni across economic, social and political spheres. Furthermore, their recognisability often extends beyond the anticipated realms of academic and intellectual dominance; these institutions are often also characterised by impressive architecture and design features situated within eye-catching campuses. They are locations that have become popular tourist destinations in their own right. Their recognisability and the aura that associates with their buildings regularly drawn upon as the backdrop for mainstream Hollywood films.

We selected four universities from the 'Super-League' for the research, we particularly wanted to explore how postgraduate students understood and experienced being in a privileged, elite university. One university in the US was a member of the Ivy League and the other a private, land-grant research university. Although they are private institutions they both receive considerable state funding for their undergraduate and postgraduate programmes. The two universities we selected in the UK are also members of the 'Super-League', high-ranking Russell Group institutions who also receive considerable state funding for their undergraduate and postgraduate programmes and are independently wealthy. All four appear in the top ten of the *QS World Rankings* (2019) and the two universities in the US each declare 25–36 billion dollars in endowments and the two universities in the UK, a total of 21 billion pounds in endowments.

Theoretical Framework

This book will draw on current debates on elites, education and inequality and consider the relevance of elite university's global brand identities. We particularly draw upon two theoretical frameworks in order to make sense of the data generated during our research. The first is Pierre Bourdieu's sociology which provides one of the most overarching and complex attempts to understand the reproduction of status and privilege. The relevance of Bourdieu's work is largely readily understandable; as the most influential sociologist of his generation he often focused on education and the role of elite schools and universities. The second theoretical framework that is used significantly throughout the book is that of critical race theory (CRT) to understand the role race and racism play in reproducing inequalities in universities. CRT is best understood as a range of approaches to understanding race and racism including some specific theoretical tools (e.g. intersectionality or interest convergence), but it is also an approach used to conduct research in which race and racism are understood to be experienced within all aspects of daily life. This book will draw on the work of Bourdieu to explore how student's *habitus* affects how they navigate the social space, the *field*, of the elite university in relation to their identity and experiences (Bourdieu, 1977; 1984; Bourdieu and Wacquant,

1992). The book will also draw on the principles of CRT to examine how universities perpetuate their eliteness through whiteness and white privilege.

Bourdieu: Habitus, Field and Capitals

Bourdieu uses a number of key terms that will be used throughout this book to understand the relationships between individuals, collective groups and institutions including field, habitus and capital. Although they may be identified as explicit definable terminology, these are terms for behaviours, characteristics and attributes understood to always be acting in relation to each other at the same time. In this sense, it is possible to think about a complex social structure, such as a university, in which individuals and institutions are always engaged in a dynamic and changing set of relationships. This is of particular significance in Bourdieu's account because it is a means of understanding and quantifying the competition between individual social actors at different moments and with ever-changing outcomes.

Bourdieu describes 'field' as the relational structures that bind institutions and their agents in continuous competition for resources and power or 'capitals' (Bourdieu and Wacquant, 1992). The field might be thought of in this sense as similar to the field on which a game is played (Calhoun, 2003), and encompassing the rules by which individual players engage with each other in their competition to win the game. However, rather than games, Bourdieu explored fields such as the field of culture (1984) or the housing market (2005) or, of particular relevance here, the field of education (Bourdieu, 1988; 1996; Bourdieu and Passeron, 1990). Within very broad categories of field there are also likely to be multiple other fields that are shaped and intersecting with the overarching field. Within the field of education we could also identify the fields of primary, secondary and higher education. Within both the field of education and the field of higher education, an individual university would be an example of a field in which individual academics and students, departments and faculties, compete for position and resources (Bourdieu, 1988). Another more specific example would be that of an elite university. For individual social actors (in the case of universities this might include students, academics, administrative staff and university managers), they all act in relation to each other by the rules governing the university field. They are also likely to be situated within other fields that may have a direct connection to the university field (e.g. sociologists and the field of sociology) or may be unrelated (e.g. practicing Catholics and the field of religion or the field of a particular church). These intersections and overlaps identify the overarching structures, often economic, that determine social organisation and referred to by Bourdieu as the *field of power* (Bourdieu, 1996; Bourdieu and Wacquant, 1992).

Within fields, individual social actors are not universally gifted the same privileges or status and, developing the notion of the field as a game, one defining feature of individual's status and relation to other actors is their competition within the field to possess and acquire capitals. Bourdieu (1986) identifies three particular forms of capital: economic capital, social capital and cultural capital. Economic capital is access to financial and economic resources and is the most readily understood form of capital that operates within the expectations of economies. Access to liquid forms of economic capital can be immediately transferrable in exchange for objects or services, whilst less liquid economic capital may be less immediately accessible but still carries its potential for transfer and exchange. Economic capital is also readily transferred within families between parents and children which can explain in part, how family wealth is an inheritable form of wealth. This account of economic activity is extended by Bourdieu in order to understand how other capitals function similarly. Social capital is a form of capital based on social networks and connections (as typified in the sentiment of *its not what you know but who you know*). Cultural capital can be identified in terms of types of knowledge including credentials (e.g. a university degree), access to high culture (e.g. visiting the opera) and ownership of cultural artefacts (e.g. a painting). Bourdieu suggests these different forms of capital circulate within economies in which there is an inevitable reproduction of inequality, one that mirrors the inheritance of financial wealth through families. Social and cultural capital can be transferred generationally in the same way that other material property or wealth can be gifted from parents to children. Different forms of capital can also be exchanged for each other. So, for example, a wealthy parent can transfer their economic capital by purchasing an elite school education for their child ensuring that they acquire higher forms of cultural capital that make them more likely to succeed in the competition for a place at an elite university. In this sense the competition for capitals within different fields is always an uneven competition in which those with greater pre-existing access to capitals are better placed to acquire more and better value capitals in the future.

Finally when understanding individuals' abilities to function within the rules of a field and compete for capitals, Bourdieu describes individual dispositions and characteristics that have been learned and practised across their life course: their *habitus*. The relational nature of an individual's habitus to field and the competition for capitals within a field are highlighted by the distinctions between different types of habitus. Some social actors (perhaps those from wealthier backgrounds who have been previously exposed to higher forms of cultural capital) are better situated to compete in a field such as that of an elite university. Whilst a less privileged student, one who perhaps has not been to an elite school and has not been exposed to higher forms of cultural capital may find themselves feeling uncomfortable and less well-prepared to compete in that environment.

The relationship between pre-existing access to resources, individual dispositions and subsequent strategies within specific fields has been shown by Bourdieu to result in fluid hierarchical structures, in which individuals continuously adopt positions of greater or lesser dominance dependent on their acquisition of capitals (Bourdieu and Wacquant, 1992). Bourdieu (1993a) describes how the fields of different institutions have their own rules reflecting their social, political and cultural histories; for elite universities this might include narratives of their origins, funding and religious affiliations as well as understandings of the types of pedagogy practised and the significance and power they may have within other fields. These fields, both the institution itself and the wider fields in which they maintain an influence, are 'a *state* of power relations' in which individuals and the institutions engage in a struggle to redistribute and accumulate capitals (Bourdieu, 1993a: 73). An individual's *habitus* are those characteristics formed within institutional struggles for capitals; shaped by institutional histories, present-day activities and the complicity of individuals who sign up to its rules (Bourdieu, 1993a).

Bourdieu notes that the 'limits of the field' is itself '*always at stake in the field itself*' (1992: 100). For ambitious, global elite universities seeking to expand their influence, the limits of the field might be determined locally, nationally and globally because of the relational and competitive nature of institutions and their agents to dominate across and through different fields. At a local level, the competition between established, traditional players (wealthy elites perhaps whose parents attended the same institutions) and newer allegiances (students from poorer or more diverse ethnic backgrounds promoting newer discourses such as 'widening participation') relates to the acquisition and redistribution of capitals within the institution. It also determines how institutions will deploy their pre-existing, highly privileged national cultural capital to acquire greater influence across global economic fields.

Critical Race Theory: Racism, Whiteness, Intersectionality and Interest Convergence

CRT scholars do not share a unifying or canonical body of scholarship that uniformly represents all their positions (Crenshaw et al., 1995; Delgado and Stefancic, 2017; Gillborn, 2018). However, CRT does always recognise the centrality of racism as manifested in the structures of institutions and seeks to 'understand how a regime of white supremacy and its subordination of people of colour have been created and maintained' (Crenshaw et al., 1995: xiii). Racism is understood to be a normal, everyday defining feature of the organisation of social life rather than something unusual or extraordinary; it is 'the usual way society does business, the common, everyday experience of most people of color' (Delgado and Stefancic, 2017: 8). CRT's earliest foundations began in the field of critical legal studies (CLS) which aimed to redress social inequalities from a left-liberal position. For CRT scholars this approach was flawed because it reduced racism to being just another materialisation of class inequality rather than identifying the specific, everyday experience of racism in all aspects of life. CRT has often been associated with specific areas of interest including education (Ladson-Billings and Tate, 1995; Tate, 1997; Ladson-Billings, 1998; Gillborn, 2008). We draw upon CRT to analyse how the centrality of racism manifested in the structures and institutions of universities affects the lives of students of colour (Perez and Solorzano, 2015). In particular three theoretical concepts drawn from CRT, 'whiteness as property', 'intersectionality' and 'interest convergence' are used to understand how the manifestation of racism within higher education policies and faculty processes (i.e. individual and collective actions) minimises the success of students of colour in elite universities.

Leonardo (2002) argues that whiteness is a world view supported and preserved through a 'collection of everyday strategies' (2002: 32) that ensure the primacy of white experience as the dominant norm (see also Frankenberg, 1993). White privilege (Bhopal, 2018; McIntosh, 1989) is the material expression of whiteness through the maintenance of power, resources, accolades and systems of support through formal institutional structures and procedures. Often the expression of the supremacy of whiteness occurs invisibly or covertly rather than as an explicitly named narrative of racist practice. The idealist expression of White privilege lies within whiteness as 'an imagined racial collective' (Leonardo, 2002: 32) that asserts a superior stance over other racial groups. The strategies identified by Leonardo are specific practices of individuals, collectives and institutions, 'characterized by the unwillingness to name the contours of racism, the avoidance of identifying with a racial experience or group, the minimization of racist legacy and other similar evasions' (2002: 32). By identifying whiteness as a property, it is possible to recognise how white groups maintain an inequitable grip on particular privileging characteristics without being challenged. The possession of whiteness as a property by white people is essentially understood to be a normative understanding of the world. It conflates status and privilege with skin colour as a means of excluding non-whites. In our analysis we demonstrate how white privilege is preserved through faculty actions and existing structural procedures within the white space of elite university fields. By doing so the exclusion or marginalisation of students of colour is understood as a normal, natural phenomenon.

Intersectionality is a model to explore how combinations of different social indicators such as race, gender, class, sexuality, age, disability and religion interact with social, political and economic factors to create moments of marginalisation and privilege, individualism and collectivism, and power and oppression (Crenshaw, 1991). The experiences of students of colour are stratified not only by race, but also by social class and gender (Bhopal, 2018; Chapman and Bhopal, 2013; Gillborn et al., 2012; Henfield et al., 2008). Intersections of race, gender and class result in different educational experiences for students of colour. In our research we use an intersectional approach to analyse such differences to explain the stratified experiences and outcomes for students of colour at elite universities.

We also use the concept of interest convergence which suggests that 'the interests of Blacks gaining racial equality have been accommodated only when they have converged with the interests of powerful Whites' (Taylor, 2009: 5). Interest convergence works from the premise that white people will only support and tolerate advances in equality for people of colour, as long as their own positions are not threatened or challenged and as long as they benefit more from such advances than people of colour. In essence, those moments of change that appear to redress racial inequalities are driven by ulterior motives that primarily provide greater benefit and security for white people. This might occur because the political stakes of ignoring racism within society become too high creating a potential more costly backlash. It might also be driven by an unrelated political or economic gain that will specifically benefit whites. During our research widening participation and the need for more inclusive approaches were a constant feature of discussions around education and higher education generally, and elite universities in particular. Interest convergence is a means of examining how such policies might overtly appear designed to redress racial inequalities in elite universities, whilst either having little or no impact in reality or providing other useful gains for white groups.

Outline of the Book

In this book we foreground the experiences of privileged graduate students in elite universities in the UK and the US and do so by exploring how privilege works to protect and reproduce privilege in elite universities. We discuss the different ways in which race and class work to disadvantage some groups by drawing on the work of Bourdieu and CRT. Each of the chapters specifically addresses themes which explore these issues.

Chapter 2: The Centrality of Elite Universities Within the Global Economy of Eliteness provides an overview of global elites. We discuss the concept of global elites and how such groups work to protect and perpetuate their own privilege. We specifically focus on how globalisation and neoliberal economies have been associated with greater private investment within traditionally state-run education practices, simultaneously matched by increasingly market-driven practice in the state sector's delivery of education (Verger et al., 2016). The chapter explores how this becomes significant for nations extending their domestic power and domination of economic fields beyond national economies into global markets (Bourdieu, 2005). The chapter argues that elite groups including elite universities play a significant role in the process of domination of subordinate national economies by wealthier, more powerful states. In particular highlighting how the high cultural capital values of some elite universities' global brands are a means of legitimating domestic political authority within global markets. As universities compete and cater for global student markets the value of cosmopolitan brands, often rooted in highly local geographies but with global recognition and reach, represents an increasingly dominant form of global cultural capital.

Chapter 3: Pathways to Elite Universities: Elite schools, Wealth and Status draws upon theoretical perspectives of Bourdieu and CRT, this chapter provides a conceptual understanding of graduate students' experiences of how they became students at elite universities. Students identified their routes to elite universities were shaped by differences in social background, access to economic, social and cultural capitals, and also by race and ethnicity. In these accounts it is apparent that the route to attending an elite university is an *exclusive* route. Wealthier and more affluent students often provided accounts of (rightly) anticipating they would always attend elite universities from an early age. Their prior experiences of attending private fee-paying schools often suggesting an intersection of interests between elite school and elite university. Less privileged or marginalised groups of students described significantly greater challenges reaching an elite university. The process of being admitted into an elite university is one that maintains the status and dominance of some groups within 'a *state* of power relations' in which individuals and the institutions engage in a struggle to redistribute and accumulate capitals (Bourdieu, 1993a: 73).

Chapter 4: Degrees of Entitlement: Who Belongs and Who Does Not? This chapter explores the experiences of students whilst attending elite universities. It focuses on students' class and family backgrounds and examines their perceptions of how this impacts their experiences of attending an elite university as a graduate student. Just as admission to an elite university was often eased by possessing greater or better forms of capitals; so to, students from wealthier, more privileged background described being at home in the field of an elite university. Their pre-existing access to capitals facilitating their experience of studying and feeling comfortable with their environment. For other students, who had not progressed along the same elite pathways, their experiences were often shaped by deficits in the forms of capital necessary to thrive in an elite university environment. Despite accessing the institution itself, poorer students often found themselves positioned as second- or third-class citizens within the university. We argue that elite universities systematically engage in delineating and demarcating hierarchies of privilege, in which students are positioned by a range of prior experiences including class, ethnicity and mobility unrelated to their academic ability.

Chapter 5: The Value of an Elite Degree. This chapter explores students' perceptions of the value of their degree and their expectations about entering the employment market. All our participants identified attending an elite university would personally benefit them whatever career path they chose to follow. They also highlighted how their access to an elite career was not uniquely premised on studying at an elite university or that there was a parity in expectations about future employment. What emerged was a systemic set of social practices in which more privileged actors were constantly being channelled towards successful future careers. The patterns of parental background, access to greater or better forms of capital, access to elite fee-paying schools identified in the previous chapters were mirrored in expectations of accessing more powerful, higher status and often globally mobile careers. The value of final degree credentials was all weighted towards advantaging a particular cohort of more privileged families to ensure their children were successful in the future. At the same time, less privileged students recognised they would benefit from their degrees but to a lesser extent.

Chapter 6: Race, Privilege and Inequality. This chapter specifically focuses on the experiences of students of colour[6] to examine how their race, class and prior experiences had an impact on attending an elite university. The chapter uses CRT to argue that white elites are produced and reproduced through systemic, structural racism within elite universities. In our research students described the detrimental impact of racism within elite universities; but also, identified a diversity of racisms determined by a range of personal attributes and contexts. This included distinctive experiences of racism for students in the US and in the UK and between home and international students. Student accounts also highlight how changing socio-economic and political conditions frame understandings of racism for both students of colour and white students. We argue that the centrality of racism within the field of elite universities is a normal, and largely taken-for-granted state of affairs; but that this is a fragmented experience. In this sense, the overarching hierarchies determined by access to capitals and habitus are further calibrated by a range of racisms.

Chapter 7: Global Brands and the Field of Elite Universities. This chapter examines the concept of global brands and how students understood the value of the 'brand' of an elite university. Whilst it is often difficult to calculate or attribute value to a brand, the students in our research identified their university brand as something that was tangible and held significant value. We discuss how the brands of elite universities are defined by shared characteristics including, exclusive admissions; the dominance of alumni across economic, social and political spheres; and public recognition. The brand is one means by which individual and collective identities, including those of graduate students, are shaped. The chapter identifies how students benefit differently from the brand value depending on their status; and, that the brand reproduces inequalities within the university. In addition the cosmopolitan nature of elite university brands are explored. We argue the local, geographical identities of elite universities are significant in terms of their global reach as a legitimising form of authority.

Chapter 8: White Capital and the Maintenance of White Supremacy. This chapter takes as its starting point the centrality of racism in the experiences of graduate students at elite universities. It explores how whiteness is a defining characteristic of elite universities, that is embedded within forms of capital that determine student outcomes. In addition, it analyses how whiteness as a form of power lies at the heart of elite universities' core structural procedures and values. It argues that whiteness is embodied as valuable within the individual characteristics of all social actors associated with elite universities, including graduate students. White forms of capitals are identified as the most valuable within the field of elite universities. Consequently, students of colour are disadvantaged because their initial lack of white capital adversely impacts their ability to compete within the elite university field. We argue that whiteness acts as a means of regulating the outcomes of elite universities in order to ensure the reproduction of white elites. Whiteness as a naturally held property of already advantaged students is also used to legitimise narratives of elite university meritocracy.

Chapter 9: Conclusions: Recognising the Unequal Field of Elite Universities. In this final chapter we consider how elite universities are premised on their possession of many shared characteristics including an apparent instinctive drive to reproduce noticeable inequalities. The chapter discusses how the recognisability of eliteness is a social construct that imbues the elite university with legitimised forms of power. Notably the nature of elite universities as producers of elite knowledge enables them to legitimise their own status within fields of education. This is a form of power that also legitimises the position of other elites in other fields such as business, politics and the media. These fields are intricately connected to elite universities because their own elite members tend to have ascended to these roles after attending an elite university. Just as the status of these universities is universally recognised, we also argue that inequalities of race and class are overtly recognisable. Elite universities serve their own interests which tend to align with white, middle-class elites; to do so they maintain regimes that reproduce pre-existing inequalities.

Notes

1   We use the term 'graduate students' in this book to refer to students who have completed their undergraduate studies and were pursuing a postgraduate qualification, typically a PhD. 'Graduate students' is the terminology most commonly used in the US. In the UK similar students would more generally be referred to as 'post-graduates' or 'post-grads'. In different contexts they might also be referred to as 'doctoral students'.
2   This claim is true but slightly obscures some details of the narrative of English universities. A number of institutions existed prior to 1,900 but only achieved university status later, for example the Universities of Birmingham and Bristol. In addition the Universities of Liverpool and Leeds were originally colleges within Victoria University (the forerunner of Manchester). For a detailed account of the history and development of universities in England and Europe, see Rüegg (2003).
3   Victoria University comprising a federation of institutions in the north-west that eventually amalgamated into the current University of Manchester.
4   Oxbridge is the name given to the universities of Oxford and Cambridge in the UK. They are the oldest and wealthiest universities in the UK and are known throughout the world.
5   The Russell Group is 24 elite universities in the UK known for their excellence in research. They regularly score highly in university league tables.
6   In this book, we use the term 'students of colour' to refer to students who identify as being from a non-white background; those who identify as Asian, Black, African American, mixed heritage and Latinx. Students of colour was a term many respondents themselves chose to use define their ethnic identities.

2

THE CENTRALITY OF ELITE UNIVERSITIES WITHIN THE GLOBAL *ECONOMY OF ELITENESS*

This chapter provides an overview of elites by discussing the concept of global elites and how such groups work to protect and perpetuate their own privilege. It specifically focuses on how globalisation and neoliberal economies have been associated with greater private investment within traditionally state-run education practices, simultaneously matched by increasingly market-driven practice in the state sector's delivery of education (Verger et al., 2016). Often the identification of which individuals or groups constitute an elite is framed within an account of their social lives or status. Whilst this might accurately amalgamate the components of elite groups and their recognisable social relations it tends to ignore the economies in which different forms of capital are exchanged in order to preserve those social relations. The accounts of postgraduate students in our research are situated within this broader context of what it means to be a member of elite groups that extend beyond just being identified as an elite student. Some participants recognised elite universities as an inevitable stepping stone in their life course; it represented an extension of prior privilege leading equally inevitably to an elite future. For other students, their encounter with an elite university represented an entrée into the possibility of a more privileged future substantially different to their past lives. These opposite poles often revealed the outcomes of very complex economies in which parents, students and universities exchanged, transferred and competed for a range of capitals (economic, social and cultural).

One of the key findings of our research is that the eliteness associated with particular universities is just one filament within a much more extensive structure of compatible attributes that determine an architecture of global power relations. The competition for capitals that resulted in our participants studying for postgraduate degrees at elite universities was a small, though we would argue very significant, part of an extensive competition amongst elite groups to maintain their elite status. One measure of the significance of elite universities within these economies is

DOI: 10.4324/9781003029922-2

their contribution to the foreign policy of their domestic interests often intent on extending power and domination of economic fields beyond national economies. Bourdieu suggests, 'the "global market" is a political creation (as the national market had been)' (2005: 225), in the sense that historically, within national economies, the extension of economic power happened along politically motivated lines that benefitted groups with greater political influence, rather than in respect of the rational distribution of wealth and profit imagined within free-market economies. And, whilst free-market economics would suggest the extension of global trade should benefit all national interests to an extent that improves conditions for all parties concerned; the same politically motivated extensions of national interests into global economies benefits, and protects, already privileged interest groups within already privileged nations, *at the expense of* less privileged nations and less privileged groups. What emerges is not just the supremacy of particular first world nations states over less successful nations, but the supremacy of exclusive elite groups within those successful nations whose power extends globally.

This chapter argues that elite universities play a significant role in the process of domination of subordinate national economies by elite groups from wealthier, more powerful states. In particular, highlighting how the high cultural capital value associated with knowledge production of some elite universities is a means of legitimising domestic political authority within global markets. In Chapter 7 we develop this argument further in relation to the work delivered through the brands of elite universities examining how the local and domestic attributes of university brands provide a means of extending the power of elite groups. As universities compete and cater for global student markets the value of cosmopolitan brands, rooted in highly local geographies but with global recognition and reach, represents an increasingly dominant form of global cultural capital. In many respects, it can be argued that the real power of elite universities lies less in respect of their readily recognised and overt generation of profit through increased international student recruitment; but rather in, their less recognised, often covert, extension of the value of their own cultural capital. Situated as elite brokers of knowledge they are legitimised in the role of deciding which forms of knowledge have the most value and the highest status as cultural capital. In effect, they have the means to validate their own elite superiority in global terms, and by doing so validate the value of their domestic interests at the expense of other national interests.

Elites and Legitimacy

Bourdieu notes that 'groups, such as social classes, are *to be made*. They are not given in "social reality"' (1989: 18) and this points to a difference between the relational intersections between individuals and institutions and the identification of their membership of a particular group. This is important for Bourdieu because it highlights a difference between the empirical evidence of group relationships and a tendency to wish a theoretical model out of such empirical observations. So, for example, in our research, there may be a temptation to identify a theoretical model that explains the materialisation of a class of elite postgraduate students and by doing so arrive at a finished typology defining different characteristic models of elite graduate students. That would be unrealistic because the empirical evidence we have gathered only relates to the relational spaces (social and geographical) occupied by a number of postgraduate students. Whilst they did often share a range of common experience, this was inevitably specific to their circumstances at a particular time in a number of individual institutional settings. It would also be a counter-productive closing down of any understanding of how elites are formed to a historical model that denied the emergence of new elites in the future. In particular our research identified experiences of non-traditional postgraduate students at elite universities (such as first-generation students from poorer backgrounds or students of colour) and seeks to explain their presence as elite students *against the odds* of their prior non-elite trajectory. The existence of non-traditional students from non-elite backgrounds is often cited as evidence of newly successful improvements to social mobility in which structural change has happened, is happening or is likely to happen in the foreseeable future. However, this is often a misunderstanding of the empirical evidence of circumstances that have happened within pre-existing social structures that reproduce similar forms of inequality over much longer time-scales. The emergence of some new elites tends to be indicative of the immutability of status of both pre-existing elites and non-elites; the short-term appearance of a change to the social structure being indicative of changes that happen because more generally they benefit the interests of the pre-existing elite. Such interest convergence has been widely evidenced in relation to policy addressing race and racism in education; most notably in Bell's (1980) analysis of the *Brown v. Board of Education* decision to end racial segregation in American schools. Bell noting that this legal judgement largely benefitted White American institutional interests, in particular redressing concerns that America's global reach was hampered in third-world countries by its reputation for domestic racism. The vested interests of elite white groups looking to extend their economic power on a global stage converging with short-term domestic policy to reduce visible inequalities echoing Bourdieu's political creation of global economies.

In Durkheim's (2014) sociological analyses of social organisation, 'elites', 'elite students' and 'elite universities' are 'social facts'; they are collective manifestations of how the social world functions, existing independently and acting as constraints on individuals. In the initial planning for this research, elite universities were identified as a recognisable feature of the higher education landscape, occupied by students and academics also identified and labelled as elite. Their relational experiences provide some evidence of the making of elites as a social fact; and in addition, that the label extends beyond the immediate field of the university. That is to say, there are other elites and often their relational experiences and interests tend to intersect. In *the making* of an elite what materialises are the processes by which they are recognised and legitimised as such; this legitimisation can be understood as the production of symbolic capital, that is of a type of cultural capital that validates knowledge (Bourdieu, 1986; 1989). Elite universities, occupying the highest positions in university hierarchies, are imbued with the greatest potential for validating their own knowledge production and consequently of confirming the legitimacy of their university's elite status. The process by which those drivers of economic and social activity result in the production of elite students is more significant a factor in understanding how elites are understood rather than the narrower framing of individual characteristics and experience. Bethany, a student at UK1, noted,

> You obviously want to separate my story from how the university runs. In principle I should never be here. The worst outcome is that my story . . . poor, working class, single parent etc becomes the story that anyone can succeed. Even if it is just that I'm here through luck. It would be wrong to even suggest that some marginal fairy tale of being in the right place at the right time democratises UK1. That's probably worse than being told I'm the cream rising to the top. Being here is none of those. It's all about being hoovered up into the scheme of things. It's matters to me and to everyone but it's totally beyond my control.

Bethany's account mirrored the identification of elites and elite universities as social facts but went further in the warning not to draw overly optimistic conclusions from experiences of successful outliers to indicate progressive social change. Bethany clearly identified commonplace narratives that normalised her personal experience; she was either the lucky beneficiary of a fairy tale or evidence of a successful trickle-down, neoliberal economy. Throughout Bourdieu's work the recognisability of social structures are identified as individual's embodiment of those structures; the structures and the perception of the structures essentially overlap. Bourdieu takes that further to make the case that the social ordering and classification of individuals and collectives are implicitly a part of the political domination of some groups by others. The perception of being dominated is understood as a natural, legitimate form of 'logical conformity' (Durkheim, 2014) in which the

> orchestration of categories of perception of the social world, which being adjusted to the divisions of the established order (and thereby to the interests of those who dominate it) and common to all minds structured in accordance with those structures, present every appearance of objective necessity.
>
> *(Bourdieu, 1984: 473)*

Bethany as a self-reflexive, individual student was perhaps at odds with the key Bourdieusian theme of implicitly recognising her position; however still articulating the collective sense that changing the status quo was *beyond her control*. This highlights the specific value of conducting this research with graduate students, particularly those who did not naturally share experiences of being the dominant class or privileged ethnic categories; by dint of time spent within the field of elite universities they often provided accounts that recognised commonly regarded as unrecognisable features of domination.

Becoming Elite: Remaining Ordinary

Whilst elites are a consistent and readily identifiable feature of social life, they can often be hard to define or categorise. Their presence within diverse fields (elites are identifiable amongst royalty, the super-rich, the politically powerful, the media, celebrities and criminal classes) all point to the construction of hierarchies as a consistent feature of different social fields. Without a hierarchy, without differentials in status, wealth or achievement, it would not be apparent that an elite existed. It is a far from original observation that the elite are only readily identifiable because they can be so easily distinguished from the ranks of the non-elite. Hierarchies also highlight the competitive nature of the different fields in which elites emerge as the competitors reaping the greatest rewards.

More significant than the simple recognition of who is and who is not a member of the elite is the account of how there might be progression; despite protesting her personal experience ran counter to the prevailing logic of elite university admission, Bethany was still a student at UK1. Often the processes of elites embracing new members are framed within a logical argument of elites adapting in order to maintain their status. A broad argument suggests that elites can renew and retrench their position by absorbing new members who bring with them useful resources. By doing so, a mutually beneficial arrangement ensues. Impoverished royalty, for example marrying entrepreneurial merchants to bring together status, respectability and unbounded wealth. Similarly, drug barons transferring, or laundering, their capital assets into reputable investments benefitting both the capital-hungry profits of investment banking and establishing credibility and respectability for formerly undesirable racketeers. More often, and as highlighted in Bethany's account, there is the suggestion that within democratic educational processes, and particularly within the assumptions of free-market economies, even if inequities persist, 'the cream will rise to the top'. These accounts acknowledge that many working-class children are disadvantaged but seemingly absolve that state of affairs by claiming the very best will always be able to make good. This is an argument that often obscures the message that an undeserving class of rich, privileged folk *need* the cream to succeed in order to benefit most effectively from their economic conditions. The logic of the free-market being that an evidential lack of skills, talent or ability of some privileged groups is likely to make their economies unprofitable and their position as an elite untenable. Problematically narratives that celebrate the cream rising to the top rarely suggest the need for a reciprocal downward mobility for individuals who might be identified as the talentless rich.

The reliability or truthfulness of such accounts often seems flawed. First, there is a discordant note in accounts of transferability of different forms of capital, the *nouveau riche* marrying into old money suggests a trade in economic for cultural capital. Whilst this exchange of capitals seems a reasonable proposition; the assumption this leads to the bestowal of elite status through a new access to cultural capital is less convincing. Such exchanges appear based on pre-existing recognition of different elite statuses. Guy Ritchie's 2019 film, *The Gentlemen*, suggested a complex web of aristocrats, career criminals, and media pundits; individually and collectively distinguished by Ritchie's characteristic delineations of classed, racial and national stereotypes, competing for status and position. In all cases the key players, be they Russian oligarchs, Jewish drug lords, American gangsters or English aristocrats, are all immediately identifiable as elite agents within their own fields. These are fields in the Bourdieusian sense of a relational network of positions occupied by individuals cognisant of the rules of the field they occupy, competing amongst each other for power and capitals, whose ability to profit or incur losses depends on their pre-existing access to capitals and their dominant or subordinate relationship within that field (Bourdieu, 2005; Wacquant, 1989). Inevitably individuals occupy more than one field simultaneously, and in *The Gentlemen*, much of the narrative tension revolves around the overlap between the field of illegal drug production and the field of aristocracy. The film portrays the competition at the borders of fields where different fields intersect and 'the homology between the specialized fields and the overall social field means that many strategies function as *double plays*' (Bourdieu, 1996: 271) in which agents' actions affect multiple fields at the same time. However, all the significant players with the potential to gain from these competitions are already dominant agents and identifiably the elite actors within their own specialised field. (Arguably the film's narrator, a duplicitous cockney journalist, is a less obvious candidate for elite membership, which might account for the casting of Hugh Grant, an actor most commonly associated with playing elite roles against type.) In essence the filmgoer is drawn into a recognition of competition amongst elites that suggests change and renewal, but this is an illusion; despite some fatal losses the dominant characters remain dominant and the dominated remain subordinated (on occasion fatally so). The narrative of *The Gentlemen* suggests a competition for power and control that is an, 'act of miscognition, implying the most absolute form of recognition of the social order' (Bourdieu, 1984: 471). Such a narrative highlights the commonalities between who are the dominant individuals within fields and also between the overarching processes and outcomes of competition within fields; as Thomson notes the,

> patterned, regular and predictable practices within each field bear striking similarities, as do the kinds of agents who are dominant in each social field. There are also relationships of exchange between fields which make them inter-dependent: for example, what kind of schooling people receive in the education field can make a lot of difference to how they are positioned in the economic field.
>
> *(2014: 68)*

A second doubt about such progression into the elite is its tendency to tap into a collective wisdom that retells myths of extreme social mobility. So, for example, the enduring popularity of fairy tales that are reimagined in new national, historical and cultural contexts but retain the same elements of social change (see Dundes, 1988, for an account of how the *Cinderella* story is not just a feature of the literary canon of different nations reinvented in different time periods but also is understood differently reflecting the social and political climate at the time). Social mobility as a realisable feature of social life premised on narratives of the poor or dispossessed elevated by luck, hard work or marriage into the upper echelons of the elite, more closely resemble fairy tales than evidencable patterns of structural change (Duggan, 2016). Examples of individual rather than collective mobility often underscore meritocratic arguments for education acting as a lever of social mobility suggesting luck (born with greater intelligence) and hard work (resilience, graft and diligence) will both reap the highest rewards. Outlining his vision for 'traditional' education in a 2013 speech to the Social Market Foundation, then Secretary of State for Education, Michael Gove, conflated elements of both fairy tale transformations, meritocratic achievement and an overt acknowledgement of the immediate potential of economic capital to privilege a child's education and career prospects. Citing the example of reality TV star Jade Goody[1] investing her new-found wealth shortly before her death into her children's education he claimed Goody understood, 'the most precious thing she could bequeath her children was not money but knowledge' (Gove, 2013). It was telling that despite his apparent desire to praise state-funded schools much of the potency of his argument (as evident in the media coverage it generated, e.g. McInerney, 2013; Walker, 2013) was premised both on the celebration of traditional public schools such as Eton and the belief that lowly individuals could transform themselves by luck or by hard work and determination. At the heart of his argument, Gove argued that 'the accumulation of cultural capital – the acquisition of knowledge – is the key to social mobility' (2013). This mirrors Bourdieu's contention that cultural capital is the most significant form of capital because it holds the key to legitimising the distribution of other capitals and recognition of status. However, it fails to address the evidence that Gove foregrounds his arguments on: That the highest forms of cultural capital are embedded in exclusive social fields that do not include state schools. Gove goes on to berate some wealthy celebrities (notably left-wing or liberal celebrities) for not sending their children to local state schools; this argument is seemingly immediately torpedoed as he notes, 'the most exclusive pre-prep and prep schools in London' chosen by such celebrities, provide a stepping stone for those children to 'move to schools like Eton and Westminster – where the medieval cloisters connect seamlessly to the corridors of power'. The patterns of distribution of cultural capital are made abundantly visible in this account; wealthy parents know they can promote their children's vested interests through particular routes through the education system. There is an intrinsic link between elite families' access to exclusive schools and their children retaining their elite status in the future. The trappings of a fairy tale like Jade Goody's story are evidence that she was an outlier; it does not provide an explanation of how to unravel the retained status of elites. Similarly, whether state schooling invests in a traditional or progressive curriculum, this is never a means of delivering upward social mobility for children from poorer families; some will undoubtably succeed under both regimes but most will always be left behind.

More generally new elites emerge from change that creates the conditions in which there is the potential to exploit a new social, political or technological landscape. This often favours groups already well-placed to advantage from unforeseen opportunities because their *habitus*, that is their dispositions and characteristics practised throughout their life course, are better aligned to the opportunities of such change. By the same token, other social actors disposed to the old routines are likely not just to miss out on new opportunities but in addition discover their habitus is no longer suited to the new social environment. Bourdieu (1977) describes a *hysteresis effect*, that is a time lag between opportunities becoming available and the *habitus* of different actors to capitalise on the opportunity. Consequently the 'hysteresis of habitus' is 'inherent in the social conditions of the reproduction of the structures in habitus, is doubtless one of the foundations of the structural lag between opportunities and the dispositions to grasp them which is the cause of missed opportunities' (Bourdieu, 1977: 83). One example cited by Bourdieu within the French academic field was the sudden changes to the economies and demographics of French higher education in the 1960s, which resulted in new pathways to a successful career in academia at the expense of academics whose habitus was constrained by the traditional rules of the field (Bourdieu, 1988; Strand and Lizardo, 2017). Another example, Mark Zuckerberg's ascension from a secure, middle-class background and Harvard University education to CEO of Facebook bears the hallmarks of hysteresis; Zuckerberg's talent and hard work is not in question but his background and status made him supremely well-positioned to benefit from the Millennial econo-techno revolution. Stone and Stone's (1984) exemplary data analysis of mid-sixteenth-century to late-nineteenth-century mobility of newly rich, successful urban entrepreneurs into established aristocratic, land and estate owning patterns of demonstrable status suggests such movement was limited. Not only did fewer rich industrialists establish themselves in the image of the pre-existing elite, many that embarked on this option later sold up their estates and returned back to the city. Tellingly, whilst mostly remaining in the city they did make 'great and successful efforts to assume a common cultural identity with the local gentry' (Stone and Stone, 1984: x). In these accounts, new elites do emerge and emerge in relation to existing elites, but the rules and markers of their standing as an elite can be differentiated from pre-existing groups. The relational nature between different elite groups follows the intersectional relation of specific fields within Bourdieu's work (Bourdieu, 2005; Wacquant, 1989) and also the overarching field of power within which all such fields are interlinked (Bourdieu, 2005).

One final example of transitions between elite and less elite status which introduced additional distinction around race and racism amongst social actors was the 2021 royal union between a British prince, Harry the Duke of Sussex and his wife, former actress Meghan Markle. A predictable pattern of convergent interests and ambitions emerged out of their different types of status. With Harry's significance as a royal player diminishing (his lineage to the throne significantly dented by his elder brother's own marriage and production of children), the couple apparently looked towards a rebranding of their status within a *nouveau* celebrity rather than traditional royal model. In the backlash of an Oprah Winfrey interview in which the traditional royal model (repeatedly labelled in the argot of TV crime drama as 'The Firm') was identified as outdated and racist, Freyne suggested this was the moment when they 'officially launched themselves in the United States' (2021: 6). In the UK the focus of the media was a frenzied debate around the place of Markle's gender and ethnicity in the context of royalty. However, a more objective view of the story's significance probably emerged outside of the UK, Freyne for example suggesting,

> this was never the story of an ungrateful pauper being elevated by the monarchy. This was about the potential union of two great houses, the Windsors and Californian Celebrity. Only one of those things has a future, and it's the one with the Netflix deal.
>
> *(2021: 6)*

It remains to be seen what significance, if any, the Markle story will have in terms of celebrity or royal futures. Of interest in the context of elite universities is how they retain their elite status and how they realign their interests in order to do so. Taking Stone's examples of British traditional landed elites and new urban moneyed elites it is worth noting that elite standing between the two retains a relationship without either necessarily superseding or vanquishing the other. Elites in this example can both be complementary and maintain their distinction. In the most recent royal storyline is both the evidence that status can go up and go down and that often it is necessary to adapt in order to maintain status or acquire new status. Elite universities pre-date the royal House of Windsor by a considerable margin and this is reflected in their general ability to maintain their elite status on a more stable footing without the need for significant course corrections

Elite Universities, Race and Racism

In fairy tales it is often suggested the spaces between elites and non-elites are complex and difficult to navigate but ultimately liminal spaces. They tend to highlight collective beliefs in which value is assigned to wealthy elites; Cinderella is not an attack on money-grubbing social climbers, rather it is the promise of success against all glass-slippered odds in ascending to princessdom. The abiding belief in such fables is hinted at by Williams account of the 'class culture gap' in the US, in which, 'the white working class resents professionals but admires the rich' (2016: 3). Williams argues that Trump's 2016 presidential success reflected a particular class-based set of valued characteristics (manliness, straight talking, rich), that appealed to working-class voters wedded to lifestyles determined by access to middle-class income levels and white skins. For these voters, elites were primarily split between good elites identified as successful and rich (and disconnected from their actual lives), as opposed to a bad elite of professionals identified as managerial, intrusive and progressive. Williams argument founders in its use of terminology (working class is effectively used to signal white middle-class interests) and by swerving the causal links of racism and poverty. She does not acknowledge, for example that white supremacy may have some direct linkage to the poverty of many people of colour and that the distinction drawn between white working class (with a middle-class income) interests and those of the impoverished may well be based on racism. However, the identification of the legitimacy gifted to some rich, white elites by a wide swathe of the population who are not in reality, represented effectively by them, flags up the effectiveness of this approach in maintaining specific elite interests along racial lines. Some of the same processes have been visible in Europe including Nigel Farage's extraordinary political successes over Brexit which at times tapped into similar nationalist and class-based interests.

Education is often associated with the power to change lives and a key component of upward social mobility. This is often premised on university's notional meritocratic function of rewarding hard work and ambition on a neutral basis that does not discriminate along class or race lines. The fairy tale element at the heart of education as a valuable public good is that it provides all students with the same opportunities to make the most of their lives. The widely evidenced reality of education as a public good is that it tends to reproduce the same inequalities generation after generation (Bourdieu and Passeron, 1979; Bowles and Gintis, 2011). Elite universities, in particular, are often identified with exclusive practices that restrict access for less affluent or privileged students. Another noticeable feature of elite universities has also been their historic ability to exclude along racial lines. This includes Ivy League universities using selection processes designed to exclude or restrict the numbers of Jewish and Black students (Burrow, 2008; Karabel, 2005). In the UK, there has been a consistent failure amongst elite universities, particularly super-elite institutions such as the Universities of Oxford and Cambridge to recruit Black and Minority Ethnic students (Bhopal, 2022; Boliver, 2013; 2016). More generally students and academics of colour consistently report experiencing racism; there is widespread evidence of awarding gaps between white and other students and academic staff are less likely to be promoted to more senior roles than their white counterparts (Bhopal, 2018).

Preserving a racial order in which whiteness is a key distinguishing feature of the elite reflects readily observable patterns of systemic racism (Feagin, 2013). It also highlights the inheritability of recognisable value associated with skin colour and how the stain of a non-white skin is recognised as a devaluing racial characteristic (Miller, 2017). Miller notes how essentially absurd and irrational ascriptions of value to whiteness are not buried in obscure or dubious literature, rather they are commonplace accounts of ethical value found 'in the most beaten treads of theoretical and folk wisdom regarding bodies and value' (2017: x). In this respect he echoes Althusser's (1971) ideological 'hailing' of the subject; individuals are recognisably positioned and their identity is accepted as natural and inevitable by those around them and by themselves. In Althusser's account universities, including the specific category of elite universities, are 'Ideological State Apparatuses' (ISAs); they act to repress through ideology. Whilst universities are understood as neutral, objective purveyors of knowledge within popular discourse; a close examination of outcomes suggests that they consistently reproduce systemic racial and class inequalities that ensure that poorer students and/or students of colour have worse life chances than their more affluent, white peers. The ascription of neutrality to the institution reflects the confidence imbued in those institutions by all social groups including those who appear most actively disadvantaged by their actions. For elite universities, the recognition of their neutral status is allied to the recognition of their greater standing as producers of knowledge; their status is conducive to the 'translation' in Latour's (1999) terms of hard scientific evidence into public discourse. Elite universities are positioned as a recognisable form of authority when accounting for the persistence of inequalities throughout education generally and within the processes of elite universities in particular. Consequently, their status means that they have an exceptional power to legitimately arbitrate on whether it is necessary to act upon evidence of racism within their own institutional domains.

Within all sectors of education there are well-established narratives highlighting race and ethnicity as key determinants of educational success. These suggest that by analysing the data about which ethnic groups are more or less likely to be successful, inequalities can be identified and redressed. However, the translation of knowledge about educational success and race is often framed within knowledge production by white interests including those of elite universities. One long-standing narrative within UK educational policy-making and discourse around educational achievement has been the claim in the UK that the groups most likely to fail are whites (Halfon, 2021). This is a fallacious argument that manipulates data demonstrating that some white working-class boys (identified through their entitlement to free school meals) do worse than most (though not all) other ethnic categories.[2] Gillborn (2012; 2018) identifies how official classification of white working class categories changes over time ensuring measurements of their underachievement remains low. This evidence derived from the specific cohort of white working class boys is then transposed across the whole of the white population to make two broad political conclusions: First, that white children are the most disadvantaged educationally and second to provide evidence that British education has performed a transformative miracle in raising the life chances of all students of colour. This latter claim is essentially a modern-day fairy tale in which education performs the role of the glass slipper. It is a fairy tale that ignores the broader evidence of educational outcomes. In particular, it ignores evidence that non-white students are more likely to attend lower status institutions, receive poorer degree outcomes than their peers and do less well when entering the employment market (Bhopal et al., 2020). Even if we were to accept the data demonstrating poorer educational outcomes for white working class boys at face value, this would still need to be offset against the abundance of evidence indicating students of colour experience worse outcomes at university and later throughout their working lives. In the context of elite universities, that is those universities that are recognised as better universities, students of colour are simply less likely to be offered a place at those institutions in the first instance.

Elite Universities

Defining what is meant by eliteness within educational contexts is problematic. Khan notes that it is 'neither enough to be highly selective, nor extremely rich to be an elite school' (2016: 175) and cites examples of selective public schools that do not attract wealthy, privileged families and private schools that despite comparatively high fees do not offer the status of elite institutions. Khan argues that it is close relations between elite families and elite schools that are essential to maintaining status. Elite universities in our research evidenced similar patterns with the parents of many students previously attending similar institutions. These family relations sat within a template of other characteristics often shared by parents and students. These included both attending the types of high-status elite schools described by Khan and students aspiring to similar high-status professions their parents already occupied. These patterns of individual, collective and institutional status mirror Bourdieu's (1984) account of the reproduction of inequalities within education. Whilst in many respects these patterns are easily identifiable, they contrast significantly against much of the discourse that defines education as meritocratic. Distinguishing empirical patterns of inequality against narratives in which such inequality is ignored or justified or simply erased from the discourse is a useful step towards understanding why inequality is repeated. It is also useful to inform understanding of the empirical evidence of inequalities of race and ethnicity that remain embedded within elite educational institutions, whilst legitimised within discourse that shifts attention from, or again erases entirely, the narrative of those inequalities.

Whilst the narratives that inform inequality within elite universities are ambiguously delineated, other aspects of how elite universities demonstrate their elite status are seemingly cast in stone. These include specific measurements of their standing on an array of global and national rankings; their ongoing connections to other, non-academic elites (e.g. politics and the media) both as a point of recruitment for their memberships and also as ongoing influencers of their current development, and, in their access to wealth. In the *State Nobility*, Bourdieu (1996) argues that social life has increasingly become organised within more complex patterns and whereas in the feudal past the church could provide legitimisation for social standing this is no longer the case. Increasingly, education is the process used to legitimise status by granting credentials to individuals. Access to universities, to the legitimacy to occupy the social spaces of elite universities in particular, and later the opportunities to transition into more rewarding and higher status employment are regulated by access to economic and cultural capital. Most entrants to elite universities require both the financial wherewithal to reach the stage of being able to apply and also to arrive at that moment in time grounded in the right forms of knowledge. One consequence of non-traditional students accessing elite universities without the anticipated requisites of enough economic and cultural capital is the reinforcement of meritocratic fairy tales. Their presence is cited as evidence that everyone has the opportunity to succeed because of greater access to a university qualification. For groups with historic vested interests in the value of a degree, such as white middle-class families who have benefitted in the past from their credentialised capital, this is both useful and problematic. The immediate benefit is that doubts about meritocracy are seemingly discounted, so the educational success of these groups is not called into question by suspicions they have privileged means to access their qualifications. At the same time however, the increasing number of graduates suggests the scarcity value of their credentials is devalued within educational economies. This devaluation is mitigated by selective procedures that ensure students from less traditional backgrounds are more likely to attend universities with lower status and by processes within universities that tend to devalue the outcomes of these students. Elite universities are demonstrable examples of these practices but more significantly, they are also the institutions best placed to legitimise a narrative that education remains a valuable public good despite its continuing inequitable redistribution of status and associated benefits to a pre-existing cohort of the already privileged. The elite university is a self-regulating system that imbues itself with the necessary symbolic capital to maintain its position, status and legitimacy.

Whilst the processes of selection ensures that legitimacy is maintained this does not disguise the ongoing competitive nature of elite universities. Individuals, departments, disciplines and institutions remain in competition with each other for resources. For elites drawing upon the symbolic capital of elite universities in a more complexly organised social world the intersections of elite interest need to be recognised and protected. Bourdieu notes the relational networks of power flowing between different types of elite family and the access they seek to specific elite schools, universities and employment outcomes to ensure patterns emerge in which the sons of industrialists are schooled and trained and legitimised to become the next generation of elite industrialists; the scions of politicians the next political class and so on. Wacquant notes that

> [b]y providing separate pathways of transmission of privilege and by recognizing competing, even antagonistic, claims to preeminence within its own order, the field of elite schools insulates and placates the various categories of inheritors of power, and ensures, better than any other device, the *pax dominorum* indispensable to the sharing of the spoils of hegemony.
>
> *(1998: xii)*

The credentialisation of status is not distributed on a level playing field throughout higher education. The increasing differentiation between the status of universities understood globally and nationally suggests dynamic adaptations to new socio-economic conditions to ensure the status quo is maintained. Attending an elite university for a working class or student of colour might represent a new and novel experience that impacts greatly on their life chances. In broader terms however, it is a mitigating rather than revolutionary factor in the social structure which remains largely unchanged. For the individual student at an elite university, it is probably not an experience that displaces or revokes their past experience. As Bourdieu suggests,

Habitus changes constantly in response to new experiences. Dispositions are subject to a kind of permanent revision, but one which is never radical, because it works on the basis of the premises established in the previous state. They are characterized by a degree of constancy and variation.

(Bourdieu, 2000: 161)

In the elite university, the habitus of non-traditional students is a disadvantageous habitus linked to less successful outcomes.

Notes

1 Jade Goody became famous when she appeared on Channel 4's reality TV programme, *Big Brother*. She was renowned for her lack of taste, loud character and racist bullying of a contestant on a subsequent celebrity series of Big Brother (Bhopal and Myers, 2008; Holmes, 2004). The Michael Gove speech deliberately engineers both the fairy-tale element of her rise to fame and tragedy of an early death (of cancer, aged 27) in relation to the financial arrangements she made for her children's education.

2 Notably pupils from Gypsy, Roma and Traveller background consistently underachieve by a considerable margin compared to all other ethnic groups.

3
PATHWAYS TO ELITE UNIVERSITIES

Elite Schools, Wealth and Status

Drawing on theoretical perspectives of Bourdieu and critical race theory (CRT), this chapter provides a conceptual understanding of graduate students' experiences of how they became students at elite universities. Bourdieu (1993a) describes how the fields of different institutions have their own rules reflecting their social, political and cultural histories. This chapter explores how the field of elite schools intersects with those of elite universities and by doing so maintains the status and dominance of some groups within 'a *state* of power relations' in which individuals and the institutions engage in a struggle to redistribute and accumulate capitals (Bourdieu, 1993a: 73). In particular it argues that the route to attending elite institutions is an *exclusive* route. In addition, this chapter explores the journeys of students from less privileged backgrounds who did not attend elite schools but were graduate students at elite universities.

There is a wide body of evidence to suggest that attending an elite school is based on access to particular types of privilege and status (Karabel, 2005; Stevens, 2007), which results in the reproduction of elites (Bourdieu, 1996; Walford, 2006). This includes analysis of social and ethnic make-up (Khan, 2011; Koh and Kenway, 2012; Weis and Cipollone, 2013), gender (Allan and Charles, 2014; Forbes and Lingard, 2013; 2015) and intersectionalities determined by gender, race and class (Epstein, 2014; Fahey, 2014; Kenway et al., 2015). Across the globe, elite schools are identified as being a gateway to ensure that privilege continues to be reinforced to create a process of upward social mobility for an exclusive cohort of students, in the UK (Zimdars et al., 2009), the US (Khan, 2011), France (Bourdieu and Passeron, 1977; Van Zanten and Maxwell, 2015), Australia (Connell et al., 1982), Ireland (Courtois, 2015), Barbados (Greenhalgh-Spencer, 2015) and Brazil (Windle and Nogueira, 2015). These patterns have been mirrored in access to international English schools (Waters and Brooks, 2015) and for second-generation migrant groups (Crul et al., 2017).

DOI: 10.4324/9781003029922-3

Whilst some students report being unaware of the privileges associated with attending elite schools (Howard, 2009; Maxwell and Aggleton, 2013) or the significance of their class background (Howard et al., 2014; Khan, 2011; Weis et al., 2014), Bourdieu argues that elite schools in France 'produce a consecrated elite' (1996: 102). They are imbued with a personal *habitus* aligned with making easy transitions to elite universities and in their later lives into elite professional employment. *Habitus* in this sense is those characteristics or dispositions formed within institutional struggles for capitals, shaped by institutional histories, present-day activities and the complicity of individuals who sign up to its rules (Bourdieu, 1993a). The elite school in this sense transforms the elite student by imbuing them with an awareness of their eliteness, 'that is not only distinct and separate, but also recognised by others and by itself as worthy of being so' (Bourdieu, 1996: 102). This consecration of students with the particular attributes of elite schools prior to university is preparation for a university experience that, in turn, channels students towards 'professions that are most appropriate for people like them' (Binder et al., 2016: 22). Binder et al. (2016) argue that college students on elite campuses arrive with 'a well-honed habitus, cultivated in similar upper and socio-economic status backgrounds, and then encounter new – but largely homologous – opportunities and discourses that trigger them to "want" the jobs being offered' (2016: 22). Whilst such processes imbue students from different backgrounds with the new identity of the university, the campus environment still plays 'a large, independent role in the production and reproduction of social inequality' (2016: 35).

Graduate students at elite universities often completed their undergraduate studies at the same or similar elite universities reflecting broader patterns of classed progression through higher education (Pásztor and Wakeling, 2018). In our research, regardless of their personal background, respondents consistently identified patterns of privilege associated with these characteristics that mirrored a Bourdieusian narrative of the reproduction of privilege. Prior access to economic, social and economic capitals benefitted students in their competition for places at elite universities (Bourdieu, 1996; Bourdieu and Passeron, 1990). The same characteristics tended to signal students whose *habitus* aligned most closely with the elite university field (Bourdieu and Wacquant, 1992) and consequently thrived in its environment.

Elite Schools: Making, Recognising and Legitimising Privilege

The parents of children who attend fee-paying, independent school often argue that they are simply choosing to invest their economic capital in their children's education. By doing so, they may claim they are *simply doing their best for their children*. Whilst it is difficult to dispute their right to use their economic capital as they see fit within a free-market economy, it is equally apparent that private schooling raises significant ethical concerns about the overt production of educational inequalities. The evidence that private, fee-paying schools produce advantageous outcomes for families with greater wealth is overwhelming (Boden et al., 2020; Cullinane, 2017; Green and Kynaston, 2019; Green et al., 2017; Lowe, 2020; Ndaji et al., 2016; Sutton Trust/Social Mobility Commission, 2019). This is even more apparent in the case of particular elite schools and elite universities. Long-standing connections between elite schools and universities have been widely cited as perpetuating access based on inequalities of wealth and power (Karabel, 2005; Zimdars, 2010; Zimdars et al., 2009). In particular a small number of largely fee-paying, elite schools have actively engaged in practice designed to ensure a disproportionately large number of their pupils attend elite universities in the UK (Elliot Major and Machin, 2018; Kynaston and Green, 2019; Reeves et al., 2017; Sutton Trust, 2011), in the US (Cookson and Persell, 1985; 2010; Mullen, 2009; Rivera, 2015) and globally (Courtois, 2017; Koh, 2014; Kenway et al., 2017). The unique selling point of many elite schools is their reputation for delivering these outcomes. The headline for a review of 'Engines of Privilege: Britain's Private School Problem' (Green and Kynaston, 2019) in *The Times* ironically noted the problem inherent in highlighting the inherent unfairness of such school,

> unjust, elitist; please let my kids in; This powerful attack on public schools ends up an unintended advert for them.
>
> *(Rifkind, 2019: 7)*

It is hard not to conclude that the overt inequality elite schools engender is readily legitimised within a broad swathe of public opinion that goes beyond the actual customers of these elite schools. Such legitimacy emphasises how certain types of inequality are almost unchallengeable; they are accepted as a matter of fact as everyday features of social life. In Weber's (1968) terms the need for legitimacy, both by the fortunate exposed to the privileging effects of an elite education and by those excluded from its benefits, often seems framed as the individual desire to come to terms with recognisable inequality. Bourdieu's (1984) analysis suggests a more recursive engagement between collective legitimisation and the structural process. Students in our research often identified both individual and collective patterns of inequitable access to elite universities, but these were often laden with both individual and collective explanatory narratives in which overt inequalities were either justified or defrayed by reference to individual, personal qualities.

In the UK the two most elite universities, Oxford and Cambridge, have been shown to have long-standing direct connections with specific fee-paying independent schools (Zimdars, 2010; Zimdars et al., 2009) including relationships with university admissions tutors who maintain significant roles as gatekeepers to these universities. Until 2018 the Master, or head, of Trinity College[1] at the University of Cambridge automatically held a seat on the board of governors at the elite private Westminster School reflecting a relationship that stretched back to the sixteenth century (Turner et al., 2021). Perhaps unsurprisingly the college has consistently made more offers of places to pupils from Westminster than any other school. Despite repeated claims that Oxford and Cambridge are addressing inequalities of access, in 2021, half of Oxford's colleges handed out the most offers to pupils from just two elite public schools: the £44,000-a-year Eton College and Westminster School, where fees are £31,500 a year for day pupils. Of Oxford's 32 colleges, nine made the highest number of offers to students from Eton and a further seven gave the most offers to those from Westminster.

(Turner et al., 2021: 10)

Oxford and Cambridge have singularly different entrance procedures to those of all other universities including traditions of distinctive interviews and entrance examinations to sift out the most suitable candidates. In addition one anomaly of the college system is that students have to be accepted by both the university and a college in order to gain admission. For students the college system retains its significance throughout their university experience, retaining responsibility for the distinctive tutorial teaching within these universities. Many state schools, however, provide little support for the specific demands of these entrance procedures and fee-paying schools pride themselves on a reputation for successfully preparing their pupils for this process which, in light of the close relationships between colleges and schools, is probably accurate. The convergence of systematic processes (different, occasionally obscure admissions rituals), close personal and institutional connections between schools and elite universities and narratives that legitimise the value of educational outcomes associated with these schools indicate a systemic, wholesale package in which families with access to capitals are legitimised to retain family status and power. There is a specificity to the form of educational economy in which the relationship between elite schools and universities is maintained, in which economic capital (school fees), cultural capital (knowledge of admissions processes) and social capital (social networks) are easily exchanged in order to bolster the pre-existing standing of all those involved (parents, students, school and universities).

In the US, admissions processes to Ivy League and other elite universities have similarly prioritised student characteristics and skill sets more likely to be fostered within elite schools and amongst more affluent families over and above academic grades. Karabel (2005) notes this practice originated in early twentieth-century Ivy League universities, in which anti-semitic admission processes were designed to exclude Jews. However, the principles of controlling against academic achievement in order to select more exclusively have since flourished in the significance accorded a range of extra-curricular activities that often require parental financial expenditure (Warikoo, 2022). Khan suggests, 'There are more wealthy children at elite schools because elite schools have developed metrics of "qualification" wherein certain qualifications can be purchased. Thereby, wealthier people have a better chance of admission' (2016: 178). In this sense, the metrics that measure educational achievement act as a means of legitimising recognition of the privileged access to better educational outcomes as a befitting conclusion to an evidentially unjust educational system. They are specifically measures of pre-existing capitals as guarantors of future privilege.

Elite Schools and the Global Educational Economy

Elite schools are widely identified as contributing to the needs of a growing global elite capitalist class (Harvey and Maclean, 2008; Robinson, 2004; Sklair, 2000) in particular catering to expectations of mobility within transnational elites (Elliott and Urry, 2010). This results in a global market of elite education which is directly linked to national markets (Kenway et al., 2013); transnational elites seeking to prepare their children for entry into mobile futures. Kenway and Fahey (2014) argue that elite schools are ahead of the game when it comes to entry to elite universities, particularly understanding specific criteria (entrance tests and interviews). 'Knowing these criteria is vital knowledge for an elite school to enable it to develop what we call its grooming curriculum, which is about hot-housing the appropriate identities and sensibilities and elite aspirations and orientations' (p. 183). This has resulted in a rise in 'shadow education' industries which help students to prepare for the admissions processes to elite universities (Bray and Lykins, 2012). Certain students have access to global connections which helps them to gain entry into elite education and elite professions. 'International employment mobility, particularly in the high-end professions is increasingly becoming a feature of the lives of the privileged' (Kenway and Fahey, 2014: 186). Kenway and Fahey (2014: 190) argue that those students who gain access to elite universities see themselves as 'the best of the best globally'. They identify as serious players within the global market, not least because they regard themselves as having more in common with a global market, that is like them, compared to a local market that is not. The alignment of characteristics and dispositions key to success within global economies of being mobile professional members of transnational corporations is imbued as a natural characteristic of attending particular schools and universities.

Forbes and Lingard (2015) have explored how gender, wealth and social class produce a particular type of privilege in elite schools which constitutes a particular habitus of 'assured optimism' in which schools become a 'forcing ground' for the 'intense cultivation' of a particular privileging habitus (p. 116). In their study, Forbes and Lingard (2015) found that the elite school privileged certain social and cultural activities which would prepare girls for their participation in global activities. They state, 'These practices are geared to the achievement of the desired cultural capital, including transnational and cosmopolitan capital and secondary habitus' (p. 126). The school itself is physically stunning and this prepares the girls at the school for their magnificent futures, so that 'physical capital is being utilised towards the (re)production for the girls not only of cultural aesthetic capital, but of intellectual academic capital' (p. 128).

Elite schools have used strategies to both try and increase their diversity but also to ensure that they are part of the global educational market (Cookson and Persell, 2010; Koh and Kenway, 2012) but it has been argued that this has been a strategy to increase their position in a globalised, competitive market (Courtois, 2015).

Consequently, there has been a shift for elite schools to focus and market themselves to a global market economy (Kenway and McCarthy, 2014; Wagner, 1998).

The Progression of Privilege: School Experiences

Many of the students who participated in our research shared readily identifiable characteristics associated with gaining admission to elite universities (Bhopal, 2018; Bhopal et al., 2020; Bourdieu, 1996; Jack, 2014; Karabel, 2005; Reay, 2017; Zimdars, 2010; Zimdars et al., 2009). Many came from relatively affluent backgrounds with parents working in high-status, professional occupations. Often their parents had previously attended similar elite universities and there was an overarching sense such students benefitted by accessing specific forms of cultural capital including knowledge about admissions processes and the expectations of elite universities when selecting candidates. Many of the same students also attended exclusive, fee-paying schools with long-standing connections to elite universities. For these more privileged students the accounts of their progression to elite universities often suggested they repeatedly benefitted from exclusive practices in which it would be almost unimaginable if they did not attend these institutions. They shared characteristics consistently identified with the progression to elite universities of students from wealthier families, in particular drawing upon long-standing connections between these universities and exclusive, fee-paying schools (Bourdieu, 1996; Karabel, 2005; Zimdars, 2010). Tony (British, US2), for example commented that he was 'always aware' of the 'names' of elite universities. He went on to explain how his personal dispositions and social background aligned with his well-founded expectations and experience of US2,

> I'm very at ease in this sort of environment. It would be odd if I felt I did not belong here. I went to [private school in UK] and to [elite UK university]. Dad went to the same school and then [UK2]. All my teachers went to Oxbridge. Literally, when I was doing my "A" Levels[2] every single one of my teachers had been to Oxford or Cambridge.

Bartholomew (British, UK2) described similar experiences to Tony. He attended a private (fee paying), selective school before completing an undergraduate degree at UK2. Describing his personal circumstances, his parents were bankers and both his brothers also attended elite universities, Bartholomew said, 'I never thought that I would not come here' and elaborated that his membership of an elite university seemed a natural continuation of his prior education,

> I have been privately educated and I know what's expected of me. There is a certain standard that's the norm and not the exception. The whole school system was set up to send us to [UK2]; interview preparation, classes to get you to say the right thing in the interview – the whole shebang!

The expectations that such privileged backgrounds prepare students for attending elite universities were also shared by American respondents. Betty (American, US1) suggested,

> If you are from a background where this is expected of you, then you go ahead and strive for it. If you come from a background where your parents are professors or work in top professions then that's what you strive for. It's just natural to want to do that.

Betty identified the privilege that characterised her educational trajectory was emphasised by the brand name of US1; noting, 'I know I'm privileged because I can say to people I am a student at US1'.

Within their explanations of their progression to becoming graduate students at elite universities, Betty, Tony and Bartholomew all identify a legitimacy to their academic success. Whilst clearly identifying narratives in which that success was fostered by privileged upbringings and framed by inequalities that only occur outside of their personal experience, they did not suggest this diminished their own achievements or their rightful entitlement to a place at an elite university. The personal characteristics and dispositions identified by these students as significant to their educational achievement can be understood in terms of *habitus*; predispositions shaped by past experiences and integral to structuring their current social world (Bourdieu, 1977) by shaping strategies to success (Bourdieu, 2008). Students' recognition of their privileged backgrounds was often openly acknowledged, but rarely framed as implicitly unjust or unfair. Rather their own success was explained within beliefs that the overarching structure of education was essentially meritocratic; consequently individual students can justify their own positions of privilege in elite schools (Howard, 2006; Maxwell and Aggleton, 2013) as less significant factors when accounting for their current success. One strategy students deployed to acknowledge their personally privileged biographies, and account for their academic achievement, was to provide narratives that consistently suggested they earned their university places based on their intelligence and hard work. Tony explained,

> I've always worked hard. Really hard. It would have been a complete waste to go to [Private school], to be quite bright and then not make the most of that. I had one big opportunity: I'm from a comfortable, middle-class family. After that it's all down to me.

Students tended to frame their narratives in terms of their personal legitimacy to attend and be associated with the name of elite universities. In this way, the brands of elite universities were closely aligned to more privileged students' educational experiences. The brand manifested as a continuation of social spaces they were comfortable working within and of constellations of attributes, skill and attitudes that their expectations of the brand. Students recognised within themselves an abundance of useful character traits, a *habitus* shaped by family and school experiences that mirrored those of the brand, but were contextualised within their own personal abilities and skills.

Unlike many other students Martin (US1) described being very comfortable with aspects of the privilege in his background that had benefitted him personally. Both his parents were British but he had grown up in both the US and the UK and attended elite fee-paying schools in both countries. He completed his undergraduate studies in UK1 and was currently completing his doctoral studies at US1. His father was a successful film producer and he described his mother by saying she, 'comes from money'. Describing his route to US1 he suggested,

> There are obvious inequalities. It's not that deep though is it? And its not that bad either? If you were in Bangladesh now or Somalia I don't think the inequalities at US1 would be that troubling. You might just want some rice and lentils on your table? There's that labelling of experience, because you went to [famous private school], because your mother is [famous aristocrat], because you spend the summer with . . . all these things get labelled as entitlement, being entitled. But in reality that's just who you are. It would not make my parents better people if they refused to invest in my education, pay for things. They would not be better parents if they sent me to a public high school with multiple shootings or whatever. Just accepting something that's rubbish doesn't make them better or particularly worthy. My family is very wealthy and they use that wealth. Which is what anybody else would do? My sister left UK1 immediately she finished a degree and is making serious money. It probably says something that I'm here now still studying?

Martin was unusual in his very vocal assertions that his easy access to a privileged education was legitimate and unquestionable. However, it was noticeable that within his narrative he still made specific claims about his academic ability to be a graduate student in comparison to his sister who entered the labour market after graduation. Martin pointed out that 'at the end of the day no one suggested I had to get a first. My dad was pretty shocked. I'm the first intellectual in the family'.

Students from private fee-paying schools or good grammar schools[3] were aware of the support and preparation they received *before* applying to the elite universities including coaching to perform well during interviews and entrance tests. For students such as Anna (British, UK2), who attended a grammar school with a record of sending its pupils to elite universities, privilege and elite universities were understood in a less comfortable fashion. Anna previously completed an undergraduate degree at UK2 and was unusual in ascribing greater significance to her privileged route,

> I went to a school that was predominantly white and middle class, it was full of students just like me. We all came from quite wealthy backgrounds. I don't think many of us were exceptionally bright, but we had the correct training

> needed to get us here. We had lots of support, small classes and extra tuition if we needed it. That's the main reason we were able to secure a place at [UK2] because we knew what to say, how to say it and what was expected of us.

Whilst many participants in our research were readily identifiable as students who benefitted from prior attendance at elite schools and who came from affluent backgrounds, other did not and their accounts often highlighted less clear-cut routes to elite universities. One such student was Keira (UK1), who described herself as working class and explained how she had grown up in an 'under privileged family, in a rural remote village in Scotland'. Her dad was a fisherman and her mum a shop assistant. She described how the support she received from her local state school had a significant impact in getting her to UK1.

> I come from a very working class background and my parents were not knowledgeable about how to get to university, let alone how to get me to UK1. It was the teachers at my school who suggested it and I think my parents were quite shocked by it, but wanted me to go. I could see from then that I was going to struggle.

Keira explained that she felt students who got to UK1 did not get there because they were 'super clever', they got there because of their background and the support they received. In her personal experience she was given the support necessary to attend an elite university (a higher ranking Russell Group) by her state school but she went on to explain this was not a foregone conclusion:

> I received a lot of support in my school. I had teachers who encouraged me and took lots of time to support me. They gave us extra lessons, they made sure we could answer exam questions perfectly and they trained us for interviews and tests to get here. I'm from a very working class background and went to my local state school – which was very good – but think about how much more support those students who went to private school get. The system is not based on how clever you are, the system is based on what support you've had and how you got here. People have different opportunities to enable them to get here.

Keira's description of the processes by which she succeeded in her education both provides evidence to support more optimistic arguments that education is (or should be) meritocratic, and also, outlines the means by which greater exposure to opportunities within elite schools might make it easier to be admitted to an elite university. In Keira's account there was a constant acknowledgement that chance played a part in her success; her attendance at a good school with teachers who guided her towards better universities and addressed her own family's lack of cultural capital (such as providing knowledge about different types of universities and their admissions processes). Keira was, however, very clear in her analysis that 'meritocracy does not exist. UK1 would like you to think that it does, but it doesn't'. In her reflective discussion of how she came to benefit from her current opportunities at UK1 (e.g. attending a good state school or being well-supported by committed teachers), she was aware that she was an outlier and that her experience could easily have been one of attending a less good state school, with less supportive teachers. In this respect Keira brutally countered some of the accounts of more affluent students who suggested the opportunities they were given by attending elite schools were tempered by their own diligence, hard work and ability,

Keira: I or we didn't have the cultural capital that I see other students here at UK1. They have that cultural capital and it feeds into their social capital. Coming from my sort of family, my background and the area I grew up in, you just don't have that kind of capital which helps you every step of the way. You can see their privilege – it bleeds down – it never stops for them, they use in every way and it starts way back when they're at school, it just continues here and you can that bleeding down.

Interviewer: Can you explain a bit what that bleeding down means?

Keira: It's something that the middle class – or upper class – students carry with them. It's part of their persona, it's unspoken but we all know what it is. It's like their entitlement that they've grown up with, not just about getting a place at UK1, I think it feeds into – or bleeds into every aspect of their lives. So it's the normal for them.

Keira's analysis, often couched in the language of a social scientist, identified very broad patterns of individual and institutional behaviours that played out throughout her lifetime and extended beyond the narrow circumstances of her university life. She also related 'bleeding down' to her understanding, and identification of, racism within UK1 suggesting there was a tendency for whiteness to be assumed as the norm. The assumptions of whiteness as normal, 'bleeding down' into understanding of which students 'naturally belong here'. She identified a range of attributes including race, wealth and social status as key markers of a UK1 student.

Another student at UK1, Bethany, also identified as working class (her dad was a plumber and her mum was a charity worker), spoke about how the support she received enabled her to come to UK1 – where she had also studied for her undergraduate degree.

In some respects it is a meritocracy because you are smart if you come here. The interview process is very rigorous, they see if you can think in a certain way – and they mould you to be that way. I think we have to trust that the system they have in place works – we have to trust that they have been doing this for hundreds of years so they must be doing it right.

Despite her respect for the institution of UK1 Bethany also described her aware-ness that students' backgrounds were often a key factor in their ability to attend the university,

> It's also important and not to be naïve and to acknowledge that the likelihood of you being here is tied to the opportunities you've had in your life – your wealth, fabulous schools, great opportunities. So these things will position you in more of an advantage – so you're not necessarily born by merit, it's not a system of merit by birth – people are fostered and taught how to be and what to do.

Bethany also went on to describe a more detailed critique of the factors that might have an influence on accessing elite universities for students from less privileged backgrounds.

> To say that everyone starts from the same starting point is simply not true. Some people have more advantages at the beginning and can get far because of that. I worked hard and had parents who valued that and sup-ported me. I didn't have a mother who was unemployed, who was an alco-holic. I didn't have to support or care for my family. So I was motivated, if I was poor I would not be motivated because I would not have the energy to work hard.

It was notable in Bethany's account that the distinction between both being privileged and not privileged was made as a starting point to under-standing the process of becoming an elite student; but, this was also contex-tualised within a range of other factors that she identified as more specific to the lived experiences of students like herself who were not privileged in the first place.

Ralf described being uncomfortable with the privilege associated with attend-ing US1. His mother was a nurse and his father was director of public health in an area close to US1. He defined himself as working class and was particularly reflex-ive about his own positioning in an elite university.

> I went to a public school in the area in which I grew up. We were an aver-age family, my dad worked himself up and my mum worked long hours as a nurse. My parents always encouraged us and supported us. But we didn't have extra tuition and anything that some of the students who come here [US1] have had. When I was accepted on the graduate programme it was a different world that I was used to. I had a personal librarian assigned to me. If I asked for a book and wasn't able to come to campus, they would send it to me FedEx so I would get it the next day. When it's offered to you on a plate, it's not something you can refuse. You know it will make a difference to your experience here.

Analysing his sense of the privilege attached to attending US1 and the discomfort that caused him, Ralf was clear that he intended to draw upon all the cultural capital the institution offered him to his future advantage.

> As a white male, I know I am in a very advantageous position here, but I also know I am perpetuating that system of privilege. But I am aware of that, I am aware of the system that exists in US1 – there is a system of elitism within elitism. US1 has its own category, and there's a self-awareness of what that category means for me. I know that I have had some knowledge which has enabled me to get here, and I know that being here, that is just the beginning. I am adding to my resources. To the resources which will stay with me and which I can take with me when I leave US1.

Conclusions

The evidence that elite schools and privileged backgrounds contribute to accessing elite universities is compelling but should be understood within much broader patterns of social reproduction. In many respects accessing an elite university is simply another stepping stone from which elite groups are able to strengthen their hold on power and status. The links between elite schools and elite universities highlight the systemic nature of privilege; elite schools are training young people to acquire forms of cultural and social capital that are ultimately not simply designed to excel in top universities but rather to excel within global economies. They are an early route through which elites will eventually access the most powerful positions within politics, governments, the media and transnational corporations (Kenway and Koh, 2013;Ye and Nylander, 2015).

Against the backdrop of more privileged routes towards elite universities, other students often face more explicit challenges based on their lack of privilege. It was noticeable that the accounts of students from less wealthy backgrounds often identify specific factors that resulted in their current success. Some, despite not being in possession of the overt privilege associated with attending an elite school with close links to elite universities, still benefitted from some of the class differentials afforded middle-class families accessing good state schools. In the UK this was particularly associated with the notion of 'good grammar' schools; state schools with a well-established reputation for academic excellence and often characterised by their middle-class, wealthier intake of pupils compared to other state schools (Cribb et al., 2013). There were also consistent accounts of the support some poorer students derived from teachers and schools committed to poorer pupils identified as academically able. In these accounts it was hard not to conclude that for poorer students from less affluent areas the possibilities to attend an elite university relied not just on their personal ability but also elements of chance throughout their schooling. This was in stark contrast to the most wealthy students who had attended elite fee-paying schools; for these students it was hard not to conclude they were always going to attend better universities regardless of their personal intellectual attributes. Their outcomes were never reliant on chance or luck to provide them a lifeline in the form of supportive, committed teachers or access to an outstanding state school.

The pathways to elite universities were shaped differently depending on social backgrounds and access to economic, social and cultural capital. In the next chapter we discuss how the access to such capitals is often intrinsic to the types of students accepted onto their programmes of study. Consequently for many students who do not progress along the elite pathways, they find their time at elite universities is shaped by deficits in the forms of capital necessary to thrive in these environments. Despite accessing the institution itself, poorer students often found themselves positioned as second-class or third-class citizens within the university. In the sense the processes by which access itself were exclusive were repeated in terms of university outcomes despite the mitigating impact of some universities seeking to widen participation.

Notes

1 Colleges at the Universities of Oxford and Cambridge are autonomous bodies within the university structure responsible for admitting pupils to the university.
2 'A' levels are advanced level subject examinations taken at age 18 in the UK and are required for university entrance.
3 Grammar schools are UK secondary schools that select pupils based on entrance examinations. There are currently 163 state-funded grammar schools in England (BBC, 2016); initially intended to foster high academic standards they became associated with reproducing existing class inequalities (Reay, 2017).

4
DEGREES OF ENTITLEMENT
Who Belongs and Who Does Not?

In the previous chapter we focused on our participants' reflections on their pathways to elite universities. We now turn our attention to their experiences whilst attending elite universities. Primarily students discussed their current roles as graduate students; however, many participants also had prior experience of undergraduate study in the same or similar institutions; and these experiences also, often shaped their narratives. This chapter focuses on students' class and family backgrounds and explores their perceptions of how this impacts upon their experiences of attending an elite university. As discussed in the previous chapter students brought a range of experience shaped by their family life and prior schooling to bear on their ability to access elite universities. Social class and family background have also been identified as significant factors in determining how comfortable students feel when they study at elite universities (Lareau, 2003; Rivera, 2015; Stevens, 2007). A distinctive feature of our findings was the patterns of privileging experience that both ensured practical access to elite universities and also positioned some students as more at ease and comfortable with such access. For students from wealthier and more affluent backgrounds this felt natural; there was an easy correlation between their expectations and experience of progressing to university. For other students from poorer, less privileged backgrounds the practical aspects of admission were harder and successful admission into elite institutions was tainted by feelings of personal discomfort. These same patterns often emerged in accounts of prior undergraduate experience suggesting that students acquisition of attributes useful to belonging within elite universities tended to diverge rather than narrow through exposure to the institution. In this sense, although less affluent students often identified the personal gains they made by attending elite universities; they were simultaneously finding themselves disadvantaged in comparison to their more affluent peers. Their accounts made visible how the progressive accrual of differing experiences seemingly widened

DOI: 10.4324/9781003029922-4

students' ability to benefit from their current study. Bourdieu (1984; 1993b) describes how social actors are complicit within their field, that is they have knowledge of the rules of the field and a 'feel' for how their social interactions with other members will be conducted. Many students gave convincing accounts of the inequalities embedded within these interactions; they were aware of the unequal pathways they and other students had taken to reach their current position. The choice for students benefitting to a lesser degree often appeared to be one in which they were complicit within regimes that despite the overt inequity of their personal experience, still offered significant future rewards. For those more affluent students who gained the most, their sense of complicity seemed wedded to their perception that they were simply reaping their natural rewards in life. The distinction between the two highlights both the myth of meritocracy within elite universities and the potential of these institutions to absorb working-class talent without reciprocating equitable rewards.

Students' Experiences of Studying at Elite Universities

Students often described how they deployed their prior knowledge and experiences of studying undergraduate degrees, also within elite universities, as a means of successfully navigating their current roles. The accounts of wealthier, more privileged students often repeated, or echoed, their explanations of how they acquired types of knowledge and skills from their families and by attending elite schools that prepared them for undergraduate study at elite institutions. Patterns of successfully accumulating higher forms of cultural capital (Bourdieu, 1986) (such as knowledge of how to conduct oneself effectively), that were specifically useful to attending an elite university were often embedded throughout more privileged students' lifetimes. These students explicitly reported using these forms of capital in their daily routines. An amalgam of 'cultural capital', consisting of knowledge of institutional practices, the expectations and preparatory training embedded within family life and credentialised capital of prior academic successes systematically legitimising their occupation of institutional spaces. To a lesser extent, students described how their social networks meant that they were well-connected to other students and academics, but primarily these forms of social capital seemed to materialise through the sense of belonging engendered by the long-standing acquisition of cultural capital. Affluent students felt at ease with other affluent students and academics, less as a result of direct pre-existing social networks (though these were also identified as significant), but more through a shared collective perception of their comfortable positioning in relation to other more privileged peers.

Quite stark differences emerged between the accounts of one of the more privileged students, Betty, and another working-class student Keira. Betty explained how she perceived being a doctoral student at US1,

> There's certain things that everyone adheres to. You are occupying a space where society tells you, and your professors tell you, is elite. I can see that when I tell people who ask me what I am studying and where, they're like

wow! That must be great and they have certain expectations of you and you automatically fit into those for everyone – for your professors and your fellow students and for everyone else.

For Betty, whose parents were both academics and who had previously attended an elite university, this seemed to be both an easy and readily understandable 'fit'. She also framed her understanding of her comfortableness within an elite university space as something broadly understood outside the university. She described how, throughout her journey to US1, she was 'always hitting my marks, proving I'm right for this. No one can question that'. This seems to reflect the patterns of individual *habitus* aligning with an institutional field identified by Bourdieu (1984; 1993b), but also hints at Betty's understanding that her perception of her standing and status within the wider world was entirely legitimate. Bourdieu outlines shared assumptions about the world as a 'matrix of all the commonplaces which find such ready acceptance because behind them lies the whole social order' (1984: 470) in which oppositions between what is considered low, dull or common and what is high, brilliant and unique are differentiated. The legitimacy of such knowledge and classifications entrenches cognitive perception of social structures in which there is a 'correspondence between social structures and mental structures, between the objective divisions of the social world' (Bourdieu, 1996: 1). In essence the elite understanding their position to be dominant, whilst the masses understand themselves to be dominated; and despite the apparent inequity within that relationship, both dominant and dominated feel capable of feeling comfortable with that state of affairs. For the dominant class it remains unthinkable that they might be undeserving of their status and the dominated believe in the justice of their position. For Betty it was entirely natural to feel she belonged within an elite space and to believe that her sense of her belonging was broadly shared by other people.

In Bourdieu's account, universities resemble 'an immense cognitive machine' (1996: 1) in which institutional processing redistributes classifications upon students based upon prior perceptions of their positioning amongst the dominant and the dominated. One impact of increasing calls for diversity in higher education has been the mounting evidence that greater numbers of students are admitted to elite universities and that these include more differentiated cohorts of students by both class and ethnicity (Hartocollis, 2021; Weale, 2020). The positive picture this data depicts unravels when considered in more detail. Much of the increased access for working class and students of colour has been through increasing numbers of these students attending 'recruiting' rather than 'selective' institutions (Bhopal, 2018; Reay, 2017). Recruiting universities in the UK are institutions that are typically undersubscribed and therefore have to recruit students during their admissions processes (for example, by offering university places during Clearing[1] to students with lower grades). Selective universities are those who are typically oversubscribed and therefore use their admissions processes to select applicants they consider most qualified and consequently excluding applicants they consider less qualified. Recruiting universities are those most often described as 'post-1992 universities', reflecting their relatively recent university status in distinction to mission groups such as the Russell Group representing the interests of longer, more established, traditional universities. The admissions processes for Russell Group universities tend to be selective rather than recruitment orientated. Post-1992 universities are often characterised as predominantly teaching rather than research-led institutions reflected in their lower status and the lower capital value associated with credentials (e.g. degrees) from these institutions. They are not institutions that are defined as elite universities. At the same time, access for students of colour has been routinely devalued within misleading accounts of *white working-class boys* suffering the most inequitable outcomes (Gillborn et al., 2021), often used as a proxy within policy and media discourse for the whole of the white working class. In addition, blatant examples of inequality persist specifically in elite universities where there has been a consistent failure to recruit a student body resembling the demographic distribution of the population (Bhopal, 2018; Warikoo, 2016). One outcome of such systemic processing is the devaluation of outcomes for students whose interests are peripheral to the privileged interests of elite universities including poorer students and those from ethnic minorities. In the context of empirical evidence that inequalities persist (Bhopal, 2018; Rivera, 2015; Stuber, 2012; Myers and Bhopal, 2021) (despite narratives of more equitable access), it is easy to imagine how students attending less elite universities become cognisant they belong and 'fit' within these institutions. For less privileged students attending elite universities their perception of belonging or fitting within an elite space is also potentially problematic.

It was perhaps unsurprising, therefore, that students from poorer backgrounds in our research, who did not share the attributes of an elite dominant class provided very different accounts to that of Betty when describing how they 'fitted' within narratives about elite universities. Keira (White Scottish, UK1) attended local state schools, her parents worked in manual labouring jobs and identified as working class. She described a significant sense of the distance between herself and the university. Like Betty, she also previously attended a prestigious Russell Group university, however hers had been a less comfortable experience,

> It's difficult for me to know how to navigate these elite spaces. It's not something I am used to. It's not just the academic spaces, it's also the social spaces. There is the pressure to do well all the time. There is the pressure to excel all the time and that's not always possible. I have feelings of imposter syndrome all the time. So, this results in a sense of having to prove myself all the time. Feelings of inferiority.

Keira overlapped concerns about intellectual or academic credibility with her discomfort in her wider social life at university; not least because she recognised that her own background did not naturally suit her to the elite university environment. She readily distinguished differences between students' 'fit' with the university based on their class identities,

It's easy to tell those who are not from upper or middle class privileged back-grounds, and which ones are trying to fit in.

The sense of *trying to fit in* did not resonate with the experiences of wealthier or more privileged students who were comfortable within the social space of their respective institutions (Bourdieu, 1984). Whilst students like Betty described their legitimate positioning, Keira openly questioned the legitimacy of her place at an elite university. The legitimisation of an individual's right to greater status is one of the key dynamics through which some cultural capital is privileged over others and reproduced intergenerationally (Bourdieu and Passeron, 1990; Bourdieu and Wacquant, 1992). For students such as Betty, their privileged cultural capital fostered and developed through parental experiences and prior schooling was given additional legitimacy through its very normality. Unable to draw upon comparable personal resources, Keira described her lack of personal legitimacy and also her recognition of other students' legitimate 'fit'. The sense of 'fit' and 'fitting in' was consistently identified by students as an element of the internal competitiveness within elite universities; adapting behaviours to 'fit in' was never a simple adoption of a new behaviour but rather realigning behaviours in a dynamic set of relations with other students. Keira described 'always having to think, almost recalibrate, where do I stand' in respect of her engagement with other students, academics or college staff. Elite universities were relational social spaces (Bourdieu, 1984; 1985) in which students' positions were never fixed but always in flux based on their pos-session of types and amounts of capital, tempered by their dispositions and chang-ing in relation to other students (whose own capitals and dispositions changed and adapted to the social space). Keira, whose access to more privileged cultural capital was limited and whose *habitus* was not shaped by prior exposure to elite experi-ences to the same extent as a student like Betty, would always be disadvantaged in the competitive positioning of such social spaces (Bourdieu, 1986). That disadvan-tage was also a process that Keira understood herself to be situated within; hence when she described *recalibrating*, she was describing the pressure of having to adjust against the flow of other, more privileged members of the university who were a dominant majority.

Keira's recalibration indicated her acceptance of social processes in which she acknowledged the legitimacy of a subordinate student experience. Students identi-fied their positioning or 'sense of one's place' (Goffman, 1951), as both a relational marker and an understanding of the legitimacy of their position within the field of elite universities. By doing so, they confirmed their acceptance of how '*at ease*' or how '*ill at ease*' they felt, was reciprocal to their successful competition for capitals. By describing their presence in terms of their legitimacy to be there, their positions and their dispositions were framed, 'as a sense of what one can or cannot "permit oneself,"' and by doing so implying, 'a tacit acceptance of one's place, a sense of limits ("that's not for the likes of us", etc.), or, which amounts to the same thing, a sense of distances, to be marked and kept, respected or expected' (Bourdieu, 1985: 728). Students' identification of the inequalities that characterised their day-to-day experience of studying at elite universities became absorbed within their personal narratives of institutional life. Despite acknowledging and identifying inequalities that personally affected their experience they learned to live with them. This phenomenon is not entirely specific to elite universities; patterns of undergraduate students identifying racism and classism as significant determining factors of educational outcomes but accepting these outcomes as natural have been evidenced across different types of universities (Bhopal et al., 2020). We described this process as a '*specialisation of consciousness*' in which students are 'conscious of the processes by which they accepted such positioning, including the limiting of potential for upward social mobility' (Bhopal et al., 2020: 1322). Institutional practices are a fixed reference point through which students' 'consciousness' of their relational positioning is the 'habitualised reconciliation of daily realities' (2020: 1323) of being a student at university, of past experience and future expectations. The institution fosters the complicity of its student population within an overarching social field that delineates status within broad pre-existing hierarchies.

The systematic processes of building reserves of capital through family and schooling often appeared to differentiate the value of contemporaneous experiences. Despite Keira's previous experience of undergraduate study at an elite university, this had not imbued her with the necessary cultural capital to feel at ease in her current role. She still described her social discomfort tied to her working-class, state school background, to suggest that she remained marginal within her current institution. She identified that her own class background would always position her in an inferior position within the university and suggested that cultural capital associated with class was instilled in students from an early age. Whereas students like Betty identified the process of attending an elite university for their undergraduate degree within the context of accruing cultural capital, Keira appeared less convinced that it had prepared her for her current role or the future. She discussed how despite her previous academic successes and admission to an elite university,

> I want to be here. I'm just not convinced anybody else agrees. My supervisors are great but apart from them I'm not sure there's another academic who would know my name.

Less privileged students often identified the value of different forms of cultural capital but even when they had access to such capital often seemed less able or adept at deploying it effectively. Ria (UK1), who was the first member of her family to attend university, made the startling admission that despite a literally unblemished record of A and A* grades in her GCSEs and A Levels, a first-class degree from UK1 and having been offered funded doctoral positions at three elite universities, she felt, 'out of my depth here'. She recognised the value her credentialised cultural capital held for elite universities but explained she would prefer 'somewhere normal, for the normal middle-class'. Ria identified a 'missing element' in her character that was not defined by academic ability but purely within her personal identity. When asked if her past record of academic success should, in principle, position her as an ideal UK1 candidate, Ria suggested,

> It's just enough to get me here. But it's never enough. To be here and to feel at ease being here. To be safe it's not enough.

Keira also identified and recognised her access to cultural capital in terms of her previous academic successes, but seemed ill at ease when called upon to use it and did not like the ways in which notions of privilege translated themselves at UK1,

> Getting here is hard enough, but once you get here you would think you were on a level playing field but it doesn't work like that. There are hierarchies of difference based on your accent and what school you went to before you came here. All the posh privately educated students know each other because they went to the same schools. So they have certain ways of behaving, doing and being.

She went on to identify processes by which UK1 perpetuated this hierarchy,

> Here the hierarchies are based on which college you're at, where you sit in the dining hall, what gown you wear when you graduate down to which degree you are doing. UK1 perpetuates that sense of hierarchy and eliteness, so what you get is a system of elites within that elite environment. Elites within elites.

Keira's willingness to identify and unpick the inequalities she readily observed was framed within an account of discomfiture felt by those who do not share the attributes of more privileged students. Despite her discomfort Keira was readily complicit in her engagement within the field; she had after all made her decision to pursue graduate studies at an elite university based on her prior experience at a Russell Group institution. This suggests both an understanding of the prevailing conditions of the field and the value she could derive from it, outstripped losses of personal comfort. Keira identified a relationship between her intelligence and her membership of the elite institution that was made uncomfortable because of her working-class background. She seemingly bought into the same legitimacy associated with the types of cultural capital derived from elite universities, but without acquiring the same sense of entitlement students from more privileged backgrounds articulated. She demonstrated an acceptance of the rules and processes of the field of her university, resulting in an individual narrative which conflated her discomfiture with the experience of university life, with her account of her lower social status and her perception of her academic skills. In an echo of Ria's assertion that her intellectual credibility was 'never enough' to fully belong, Keira described not always being able to 'excel' rather than not being intelligent 'enough' to summarise her positioning within UK1. In the context of UK1, and other elite universities, *excelling* is almost the expected outcome; for Keira the inability to excel was grounded in her lack of social belonging rather than in her intellectual ability or capacity for hard work. More privileged students like Betty, invariably identified their educational trajectories as evidence that they excelled and evidenced this in relation to their intellect and track record of hard work. In effect Keira shared all these same traits but her status in the university was devalued through her perception of her background and social class.

One student who, unusually, challenged many elements of the orthodox view of elite universities as meritocratic places, fostering the most academically able students, in a very overt fashion was Femi (Black British, UK2). She did not believe that elite universities were populated by those who were the most intelligent. Femi was from a single-parent family, grew up in a council house[2] and attended her local school which 'was a crap school, we never had any resources for anything'. She argued that,

> I don't think these universities are full of smart people. That's bullshit! Most of the students have had an advantageous starting point. They've had more support to get them here, they've been to private [fee paying] schools, they've had tutoring, coaching to prepare them for the interviews and tests to get here. They have been told by everyone it's their right to go to an elite university – they are being prepared to ensure they occupy that elite place because it's their right to be there.

Despite her rejection of the meritocratic arguments of her middle-class peers, Femi still actively engaged within the elite university field and had previously attended UK2 as an undergraduate. Both Femi, and to a lesser extent Keira, identified inconsistencies in the legitimising narratives that elite universities were populated by elite students (Femi in terms of both intelligence and belonging; Keira in terms of belonging); but both also appeared capable of working around these on a personal level. Most of the students we interviewed valued their experiences of being in an elite environment and contextualised its value in terms of their own and their peer's intelligence. Unlike Femi, for most less privileged students, there was a sense that if the substantive intellectual qualities of elite university students were challenged this potentially brought their own status into question. By doing so, their interests were further entwined with their institutional narrative; they were invested in the social perceptions of belonging and not belonging, despite the apparent inequity that was associated with identifying as poorer, less affluent or working class.

Betty commented on how being surrounded by other smart students pushed her academically and intellectually; and related this to the specific social structure and social spaces of US1;

> Coming here to [US1] gives you access to exclusive spaces, which leads to other exclusive spaces. This space has a hierarchy based on how intelligent and interesting you are. I am surrounded by very smart people who

are super driven, super interesting, super ambitious, have rigour and are just kick ass smart!

Whilst Betty went on to suggest in the future her education would inform her ability to challenge the societal inequalities she benefitted from; her linkage of the exclusivity of spaces and intellectual development raises many problematic questions about the potential for social change led by elite universities. Not least the relationship between the local spaces of universities, their intensive local intellectual cultures and the evidence of more affluent students comfortably being funnelled through these environments suggests their exclusivity is designed to resist more equitable outcomes. Another student who expressed similar sentiments about hoping to challenge inequities in the future and also commented on the spatial aspects of elite universities was Amy (White British, UK2). Both her parents had previously graduated from university and Amy noted how she had benefitted from attending a very good local state school in an affluent area. In particular she described how her school had prepared her for the transition to an elite university,

> I have been taught to be confident, to sell myself and not to be intimidated by this environment; the grand buildings, the exceptionally clever professors and the smart students. This is not alien to my previous experiences so I can fit in and use those advantages. Being here. Being smart. It sounds arrogant but I can make a difference.

Within their shifting patterns of perceptions of intelligence and perceptions of belonging, many students identified that elite universities are clearly premised on perpetuating inequalities. The orthodoxies surrounding who was at elite universities and how they got there were often described in terms that began to question institutional legitimacy; but rarely to cast the whole structure into question. Students identified that they might feel more or less comfortable in the spaces of elite universities based on their backgrounds; those from privileged backgrounds feeling more comfortable than those less privileged. However, very few students identified disparities in intelligence as a distinguishing factor; the assumption was largely that all students at elite universities were demonstrably very intelligent. Femi was unusual in identifying a whole range of possible positions could be occupied within the university determined by both a perception of a student's varying intelligence and also their relative privilege. She explicitly noted that her experience was shaped by being the daughter of a single mother and argued that inequalities in society around class, poverty and race all materialised in the field of elite universities,

> It is just a microcosm. And because its [UK2]. That name. It is loaded towards certain people. But those are the same people who always do well in any situation.

For other students, including Keira who shared some of Femi's own background characteristics, although privilege was an important variable and one that contributes to how students feel about attending elite universities, it was based on an assumption that however unfair the process of getting there, being at an elite university conferred recognition of personal ability.

Performing Privilege, Performing Whiteness

Complicity with institutional narratives also materialised in accounts of how students performed their roles as elite university students. Performativity in education has largely been understood as a consequence of neoliberal economies changing the identities of educators from agentic purveyors of education as a public good, to performing to fulfil market-orientated targets (Ball, 2003; 2012). Accounts of performativity in educational settings often draw upon Lyotard's (1984) analysis of society's increasing obsession with the optimisation of efficiency that can be effectively measured and Foucault's (1973; 1977) account of self-disciplinary regimes and surveillance. Performativity in these terms is understood as individual educators internalising the demands of league tables, accountability assessments, school inspections or policy targets within their practice and a consequent loss of agency. Ball notes performativity does 'not just to refer to systems of performance management or the deployment of performance indicators but rather to the complex and powerful relationships between such indicators and management systems and teacher identity and professionalism' (2016: 1052). Macfarlane (2015) suggests that similar patterns of student performativity also emerge in part because performative pedagogies of educators require students to adopt characteristic traits that fulfil the demands of neoliberal universities to evidence their accountability by meeting market targets (e.g. better grades, higher completion rates or more employable students). Macfarlane identifies how student performativity emerges in *presenteeism*, increasing requirements for students to be recorded as present during teaching sessions; *learnerism*, typically pedagogy that requires students to publicly perform learning behaviours that align with student-centred learning approaches; and, *soulcraft*, students' ability to display their adoption of normative citizenship values promoted by the university. The students in our research did not discuss performativity in these specific formations which tend to resonate more closely with undergraduate experience but they did describe aspects of performative behaviour determined by their institutional settings. The *ethos* of their respective elite universities required particular performative practice in order to signal their abidance by the outcomes of their institution. The systematic processes by which they were assessed and measured within elite universities were differently constituted than those shaping academics or undergraduate students, but were similarly making demands on their identity formation as elite students within the local ethos and expectations of their respective universities. In these processes students' identities were often performed against an ideal or normalised student identity which was white and middle-class.

Andrew (UK2) was from a mixed white/Black background at UK2, both his parents were professional and he defined himself as 'upper middle class'. He described how the performance of privilege was used as a means of control that *kept people in their place.*

> The way that the privilege works is part of the whole experience of being here. At [UK2]. It means that there are unspoken rules that we know we have to adhere to, so that we fit in. This goes down to the college that you're in, who your friends are and what your professors think of you. It also means that in everything you do, that privilege is there and it's something that you have to conform to. If you want to be successful, you have to be ahead of the game – that means being part of the UK2 system.

Andrew expanded on his discussion of privilege by explaining that despite the advantages he personally benefitted from, including his family background and previous educational opportunities, his ethnicity still counted against him. He explained that he was conscious of fulfilling the roles expected of a white middle-class student at UK2, but that,

> You are allowed to be a member of the club, but you can't really be a fully-fledged member. By virtue of your ethnicity you are an outsider. But the college and the university likes you to think you are a full member, but in reality you are not and never will be. But, and this is the biggest but of all, you do have to make the effort to appear as though you are a member!

In Andrew's account, privilege was sharply delineated by both class and ethnicity and he felt he was required to perform such delineations as normalised conventions. Andrew identified that in some respects his middle-class background meant that he was better positioned than other students but this was hampered by his dual heritage. He also made the point that for other students who were both working class and students of colour, UK2 could be 'an oppressive space'. He argued that certain types of behaviour were expected by academics which normalised identity based on white middle-class attributes. Students who did not exhibit those behaviours effectively self-identified as being outside of the normal categories of belonging to elite university spaces. To compound such discomfort, there was still an expectation of performing the ethos of the elite university; in a sense almost identifying the personal, individual failure to sit neatly within the anticipated role of a UK2 student. In Andrew's account privilege was performed by students in order to signal they belonged and simultaneously as a means of excluding other students.

> It is the way certain types of behaviours become accepted. Being a certain way which relates to how you are seen and how your professors see you. It puts you in a certain position which says you can do this and you can do that. You can belong and you can't belong. All the time, there is the knowledge

that you and others have of knowing that you are in the space which is privileged but you should be worthy and grateful to be there.

Tony who studied at US1 shared several characteristics with Andrew. He was from a middle-class background with parents who were both professionals. He also spoke about how certain behaviours were related to his race in relation to how privilege manifested at an elite university. In Tony's account there was a significant emphasis on the need for him to adapt or conform to the US2 ethos, again hinting at the need to shape his identity within institutional expectations.

> It is clear I am a Black man from a middle class family, and I know that coming here to US2 makes me part of that privileged elite because not every Black male will have the opportunities that I have had. But you adapt once you're here. You know there's ways of behaving that are acceptable and you have to conform to that. Part of being here, is also about where the experience takes you. If you do well at US2, you will do well later on in life. Conforming is part of that process of acceptance at US2. US2 prides itself on the student experience and you have to conform to that.

In many respects both Tony and Andrew hint towards the production of a self that aligns with their university but seems at odds with their confident understandings of their own identities. Tony made the point that the benefits associated with studying at an elite university were hugely valuable and calculated that value would seemingly offset concerns about the requirement to 'conform'. Within that calculation, however, there is a clear signal that Tony revokes parts of his identity. For some students, the distance they had to travel in order to reconcile the value of being at an elite university against the demands it placed on their identity seemed greater still. Sarah was from a Latina background and identified as working class with neither of her parents previously going to university. She relied heavily on scholarships when she was an undergraduate and family support as a postgraduate student. Her parents had saved for years in order to support her to study at US1 and it was a source of great pride to them to say their daughter was attending one of the most prestigious universities in the world.

> When I am here, I know that I shouldn't really be here. I kind of have an imposter syndrome but I learn to behave in a certain way so that I can be one of them. Outwardly I could be rich and middle class. Nobody would need to know about my background. They would know because I am here, I am worthy of being here. So I can hide that I am poor and working class and that my parents have saved for years for my education and have gotten into debt because they want me to do well.

Sarah's experience of 'passing' was unusual, but not unique, amongst other students from working class and less affluent backgrounds. She felt she could hide aspects of her life and pass as being a student who was middle class and wealthy. Describing her relationship with her parents it became clear Sarah felt increasingly uncomfortable trying to balance her family's pride in her achievements with the doubts she felt about her entitlement to attend US2. She spoke about being the daughter of immigrants and 'not wanting to let her parents down' but also of the intense pressure she felt when returning home,

> It's mentioned all the time by my family, my neighbours and all my cousins. Back home, everyone says you're at US2. Wow! So you'll be fine when you finish there. It's a big deal for me being here. I know as immigrants my parents came here with nothing – but they want so much more for us. I could never go back home and tell my parents I am struggling, that would mean I have failed and let them down.

For Sarah passing was a strategy by which she could perform the attributes of a more typical, successful student at US2. It was a means of aligning her identity within the elite institutional ethos and expectations. However, much like Tony, she appeared to have lost some of her own identity in the process and seemed distanced from the identity she shared with her family. Noticeably, Sarah was a student who associated feelings of not belonging or not fitting in with the institution with an account of being less able academically,

> I pretend here [at US2] to the extent that I am one of them [middle class, wealthy students]. I feel intimidated in the classes. I feel insecure. I am surrounded by lots of very smart people. But I try and be like them on the outside, I try and pretend I'm as smart as they are. I even pretend to my advisors and professors.

The performativity of pretending to be like her wealthier, middle-class peers seemed associated with Sarah's identification of White, wealthy students inherent intellectual ability. Despite making the point that by the very fact of her being accepted to study at US2 and despite the evidence of her prior academic achievement, Sarah seemed to believe her ethnicity and her class background limited her own ability. In many respects elite universities are less constrained by the limitations of performativity related to pedagogic practice or measurement within league tables. By their very nature they already excel within these measurements. What emerged in our research was a similar though slightly different types of performativity in which hierarchies of privilege were being categorised by personal attributes. The targets imposed on students and the measures of their efficient belonging within elite universities were shaped by institutional demands privileging some students above others. For all students, including those most uncomfortable within the strata of privilege that materialised, there remained a requirement to believe to some extent in the logic of its demarcations.

International Students

In some respects the experiences of international students often mirrored those of home students. They also highlighted similar distinctions around affluence and ethnicity that shaped their experiences of elite universities. Elite universities are often linked to the emergence of global elites who share expectations of mobility within their university education and later career aspirations (Myers and Bhopal, 2021; Rivera, 2015). In this sense, very affluent students who were already exhibiting the characteristics of an international mobile elite held a seemingly natural fit with these institutions. Their accounts of accumulating capitals prior to attending university and later as international students studying undergraduate degrees often matched by their ambitions for moving into prestigious career paths that were not constrained by borders. So, for example, Christopher (UK2) was a Swiss national but had lived with his parents in Europe and America. He identified both his own parents' experience of mobility, largely determined by his father's employment as an investment banker, who at different times was based in Europe, America and Asia; and also his own experiences of mobility as a student. One consequence of his parental background was his attendance at elite private schools in America and the UK, as well as spending time at international boarding schools in Switzerland, France and Spain. He completed his undergraduate studies at an elite university in the US. Christopher noted,

> I speak French, Spanish, Italian and Arabic fluently. It's a consequence of my life. When I went to [elite international school] we all spoke different languages. It's a privilege to always be amongst people with that outlook. Some of the other students here. The British students can be very parochial. They have a very narrow outlook. They are always amazed that you speak another language or lived in another place. I avoid them if I can.

Christopher described how he felt comfortable at UK2 in part because he could mix with other students who shared similar experiences and backgrounds. When distinguishing his personal experiences from other students at UK2, in particular home students, he suggested that there was a specific niche for students like himself within elite universities. His narrative included many similarities with those of other more privileged students' progression from schools and families that had prepared them for the experience of an elite university. In addition, he also described a pattern of very exclusive networks that found a home in the spaces of elite universities,

> At UK2 there are quite a few very familiar faces. Friends from different places. Mostly friends of friends. We all seem to have been drawn here. I was

thinking about how few friends I have made here because I already have my circle.

Asked whether or not he felt he belonged he suggested that was, 'complicated, a very complex equation', and explained how his own circle of friends were always at ease with the social life of being at UK2 but that they were separated from the broader pool of other students. He very carefully explained how completing a PhD in economics was both related to realising his ambitions for the future (a career in politics), and a normal continuation of his prior social life. If he had not chosen to study for a postgraduate degree then he suggested he would have entered another field of work (politics, banking, state administration were all proffered as likely options), in which his social connections and life would largely have mirrored his current activities outside of postgraduate study. Christopher described his awareness of his privilege and his access to exceptional wealth and also identified that he was very hard working and driven; taking all his circumstances together his account of UK2 was that it was 'a natural environment' for him to occupy.

Christopher's experience were shaped within a highly exclusive mix of mobility and wealth. Other international students tended to identify some similarities but often pitched within less exclusive networks of privilege and wealth. The significance of mobility and the global transferability of elite university experiences and degree credentials was still understood but at a less rarefied level. Jane (White British, US1) whose parents were both professors had completed her bachelor's degree at UK1 and felt this experience prepared her as an international student at US1.

> The knowledge that you've gained from your previous degree at an [elite] university prepares you for your time here, because you know how to behave and what that behaviour entails in terms of getting access to networks and the things that you need to succeed.

Another international student Gargi (Indian, UK2) previously attended an elite university in the US and was now studying at UK2. Both her parents had attended elite universities in India and her father was a successful, prominent lawyer in India. She reiterated similar sentiments to Jane suggesting that there was a similarity of experience between the US and the UK institutions that were readily transferrable,

> Going to an Ivy League university meant I knew what to expect when I came here, it kind of seemed natural to me and I knew it would open up vast opportunities for me and it would enable me to have a certain kind of privilege that I could draw on to make those right connections that would work for me.

Both Jane and Gargi seemed comfortable deploying the cultural capital they had already accumulated within elite universities. They displayed knowledge of their positioning within elite universities and were comfortable adapting to the new global contexts. Gargi described particular issues that she encountered about her ethnicity (discussed in Chapter 6) which again tended to mirror the experiences of other middle-class students of colour who were home students such as Andrew and Tony.

Conclusions: Belonging and Privilege

Although the ethos of elite universities were identifiably constituted within their local practices, they also connected to wider national and global networks in which privilege was actively fostered. In the accounts of our students, elite universities were systematically engaged in delineating and demarcating hierarchies of privilege. Consequently, different students found themselves positioned by a range of prior experiences including class, ethnicity and mobility unrelated to their academic ability. The intersections of these markers of position were highly complex and to a large extent defeated the notion of identifying typologies of students. Individual students were effectively positioned across a diverse range of discrete positions rather than in broad bands of shared experience. The outcome of this positioning within hierarchies determined by pre-existing access to forms of capitals, in particular to cultural capital that can be defined as privilege, was often spoken about in terms of feelings of belonging or not belonging within the institutional structures. This highlights how elite universities shape identities in their own image. Even students who were at the lower levels of the overarching hierarchy produced narratives in which the overriding value of an elite university credential trumped their experiences of discomfort. In this way, their identities adapted to degrees of complicity with the ethos of elite universities even when identifying their personal opposition to those practices.

Notes

1 'Clearing' happens during the period between the announcement of A level results and the beginning of the next academic year (typically between July and October). It allows students to apply for unfilled places at universities. Often, the grades accepted during clearing are lower than those originally published by universities as typical entrance requirements.
2 'Council house' refers to government-owned social housing in the UK.

5

THE VALUE OF AN ELITE DEGREE

Throughout our research participants described their different personal journeys to becoming graduate students and their different experiences of belonging within elite universities. One generally shared perception amongst all students was their belief that completing graduate degrees in these elite universities would be hugely beneficial to their futures. Some students did, however, identify that this was a far more difficult challenge than for others and suggested that the scale of reward from their study would be less than that of other students. Students whose *habitus* aligned with the field of an elite university (Bourdieu, 1984; 1993b), generally those from wealthier, more privileged backgrounds who had attended private schools, often felt destined to benefit to a greater extent. They were also identified by many other students better positioned to reap the greatest rewards and of possessing a readier form of accessibility to the potential advantages of an elite degree. Despite the apparent unfairness of these competitive relations, students who were less well-placed still described their recognition of the value that attending an elite university would accrue to themselves. The lesser value they identified was still significant enough to ensure that they remained committed to the process; indicating that in a Bourdieusian sense they were readily complicit with the rules of the field for relatively unsubtle economic reasons. Complicity was understood to be readily rewarded in the near future in the employment market. All students identified that attending an elite university was considered a stepping stone in their lives directly linked to achieving greater success in the future. Most students suggested that it would result in their successful progression into rewarding, well-paid, elite jobs. Ralf noted both the status associated with being at US1 and identified wanting to 'get what I can from it',

> Once you have [US1] on your *resume* you're gold and sorted. By being here, you are occupying a certain place in society, it's a place where you either sink

DOI: 10.4324/9781003029922-5

or swim. If you are taught it's your right to be here, then you will swim. You are already occupying a space in society that says you have a right to be here and the university tells you that in the way that it operates.

Ralf explained that his own background (he previously attended a public school and his parents both worked in public healthcare) did not align his interests with more privileged US1 students. He was explicitly aware of the inequities US1 fostered and reproduced; however, he explained that his own, equally explicit, practice was to ensure that he personally derived as much value as possible from the university. Keira was unusual amongst the students we interviewed because she expressed her disappointment with students who simply understood the acquisition of elite university credentials in terms of economic rewards,

> You can get lost in a corporate bubble here, a lot of the students say they want to earn over 50k [£50,000, UK sterling] as their first job and a lot of them go on to do that after they graduate. For most of them that is their aim and they can use the name [of the university] to get them there. It makes me think of the value of what they have learnt. Is it learning for learning's sake? Just to get a well-paid job at the end of it, or is it something more than that?

Keira appeared to identify the potential of elite universities to be more than a simple engine to reproduce inequality, however her own discomfort based on her class background was in stark contrast to the 'sink or swim' approach of Ralf. Despite their different approaches, both Ralf and Keira appeared to suggest that elite universities were specifically effective in promoting the interests of students who were comfortable with their privilege.

The Value of Degrees

Ralf and Keira's understanding that elite university degrees have a direct correlation to greater earnings is unsurprising and reflects well-established principles about educational outcomes and affluence. The value of a degree is widely identified in terms of the economic value it adds to a student's future life chances (Reeves et al., 2017). In the UK the Institute for Fiscal Studies (IFS) has repeatedly monitored graduate earnings and found a net positive gain in lifetime earnings even when comparing graduates and non-graduates with similar characteristics (e.g. prior academic achievement at age 18), and when allowing for the costs of student loans and impact of progressive tax regimes on higher earners (IFS, 2020). The IFS noted variations within these outcomes including by subject area, by gender (men generally earning more than women) and by types of universities such as the Russell Group which were also associated with higher earnings. Similar patterns of lifetime earning amongst graduates and non-graduates have also been identified in the US (Tamborini et al., 2015). Postgraduate degrees (master's and PhDs) in the UK have been identified as generally associated with higher earnings than undergraduate degrees, although this is not the case for Postgraduate Certificates in Education (PGCEs) which are used as an entry point to becoming a teacher (DfE, 2020). In the US postgraduate degrees have also been linked to higher earnings (Tamborini et al., 2015).

In addition and related to the potential for higher earning, elite universities are understood to funnel their students into particular types of employment often associated with status and power (Reeves et al., 2017; Rivera, 2015). One notable example is the very high numbers of former Oxbridge students who enter the UK parliament as MPs from all political parties. In 2019 just under half (48%) of all cabinet ministers attended Oxbridge, and of 33 cabinet ministers, only ten had not completed undergraduate degrees at Russell Group universities (Sutton Trust, 2019). The same report also noted that almost two-thirds of the cabinet attended independent, fee-paying schools. In 2019 the Sutton Trust (Sutton Trust/ Social Mobility Commission 2019) found that despite 'isolated pockets of positive change' the UK remained 'a country whose power structures are dominated by a narrow section of the population' (2019b: 4). In particular they noted the 'media, alongside politics and the civil service, form a triumvirate of sectors at the top of the socially exclusive list' (2019b: 4). With less than 1% of students studying at Oxbridge it is staggering that 24% of all MPs (including 57% of cabinet ministers), 56% of Permanent Secretaries, 71% of senior judges, 44% of newspaper column- ists and 31% of BBC executives all emerged from these two most elite universities. The Sutton Trust (2019) also highlighted that amongst these same groups, 29% of MPs (39% of cabinet ministers), 59% of Permanent Secretaries, 65% of senior judges, 44% of newspaper columnists and 29% of BBC executives also attended independent schools underlining the consistent patterns in which privilege is fos- tered and channelled into high-paying and powerful roles in society. As discussed in Chapter 3 elite schools are one means by which wealthy families can strategically deploy their economic capital to ensure that their children are likely to succeed in the future. There is a seeming inevitability that 'Children from families at the top of the economic hierarchy monopolise access to good schools, prestigious uni- versities and high paying jobs' (Rivera, 2015: 1). Elite universities being the final significant conduit in which family wealth and access to privileged forms of edu- cation are translated into specifically valuable employment opportunities (Mettler, 2014; Owens and Rivera, 2014; Rivera, 2015). The value of these roles in poli- tics, government or the media is particularly significant because they place already advantaged actors in positions that will enable them to shape how inequalities can be maintained. Whilst politicians, senior civil servants and the upper echelons of transnational corporate bodies are well-placed to enact inequalities; the presence of a sympathetic choir of media voices acting as a legitimising authority ensures the successful compounding of structural inequalities and perceptions of the unchal- lengeable efficacy of their existence.

Rivera (2015) argues that through a process of overt selection in the hiring process, students from prestigious universities are allocated top jobs based on their parents' wealth and socio-economic backgrounds. Simply attending an elite university is one, but not the only, key determinant in accessing the *most elite*, well-rewarded positions. Rather, attending an elite university is one element in a systematic set of processes that ensures privilege is transmitted generationally. Education is a significant conduit because elite universities are the stage in which access to the job market and a direct means of accessing wealth in the future materialise as real-life rewards. Parents from wealthier backgrounds are able to invest in their children's education, through school choice and then by attending an elite university (Friedman, 2013), which inevitably ensure that their children also have access to economic resources with which to promote their future interests. Allied to the specific transmission of economic capital, wealthier, more privileged parents are also able to draw upon a range of other resources that add to the value of their children attending elite universities. They are able to use access to social networks which have a significant impact on young people's confidence when navigating the spaces of elite universities (Coleman, 1988; Linn, 1999) and access to cultural resources, capitals and networks (Lamont and Lareau, 1988). Lamont (1992) argues that 'symbolic boundaries' influence how different groups are separated by different inequalities, and Rivera suggests that these symbolic boundaries, 'influence to whom we devote time and attention and include or exclude from our social networks. Consequently, class influences whom we choose as friends, neighbours, spouses and . . . new hires' (2015: 8). When accessing the job market, all students benefitted by attending an elite university but this needs to be qualified by processes in which more privileged students were able to benefit more easily and at the same time benefit to a greater extent than their less privileged peers.

As discussed in Chapter 3, many of our students identified inequitable admissions process at elite universities that benefitted them personally but justified their own success in terms of personal ability, hard work and merit. By doing so, they provided narratives in which their perception of their positioning within an inequitable process remained justified and they were comfortable that their personal rewards were well-earned. Rivera argues that merit is 'a social construction embedded in societal-level cultural beliefs about what constitutes worth in a given time and place' (2015: 9). She further argues that merit is based on and directly linked to the values and qualities of elite groups who 'generally control society's gatekeeping institutions and thus have the power to shape what merit is and how it is measured in a given domain' (2015: 9) (see also Bourdieu, 1984; 1993b). Elite universities, through a range of practices (including admissions; long-standing social networks with particular elite schools and powerful, high-status professions; and, through the expectation of specific norms of social behaviour from students), enforce both the reproduction of inequality and simultaneously legitimise the process and its culture. Rivera states,

> Culture affects elite reproduction, not only by shaping individual's aspirations, values and behaviour along with how they are judged in everyday social interactions, but also by dictating how the gatekeepers that control

access to positions of power, prestige and pay define merit and allocate valued resources.

(2015: 10)

In her research, Lareau (2003) examined how parents from privileged backgrounds developed a 'concerted cultivation' approach towards their children's upbringing. Parents use their skills to navigate schools to the advantage of their children as well as making sure that their children were participating in structured and measured extra-curricular activities outside of school. Consequently, this approach had a significant impact on student achievement and future success. Stevens (2007) argues that parents of such children are better placed to navigate the admissions system into elite universities. Their approach to their children's education means that they are able to prepare their children for tests and interviews (both through their knowledge and access to wealth), more effectively than parents of similarly capable children from less affluent backgrounds. Cultural capital in the form of knowledge about *how education works* is heavily loaded in favour of more privileged families who have previously benefitted from its inherent inequalities. As Stevens highlights, the 'ability to assemble a strong [university] application is not evenly distributed across the population. Those without an inkling of how decisions are made by admissions officers are at a distinct disadvantage' (2007: 21).

Students who attend elite universities develop clear understandings of their destinations after graduating and tend to be highly selective in their choice of careers, focusing on those which have prestige and high earning potential (Binder et al., 2016; Khan, 2012). Rivera (2015) found that earning a six-figure sum was seen as an indication of personal success and that at Harvard University, '*over 70 percent of each senior class* typically applies to investment banks or consulting firms through on-campus recruitment' (Rivera, 2015: 56) (see also Lemann, 1999). Students at elite universities are able to distinguish between 'high status' and 'ordinary jobs', not least because, 'status processes on college campuses are central in generating preferences for the uppermost positions in the occupational structure and that elite campus environments have a large, independent role in the production and reproduction of social inequality' (Binder et al., 2016: 20). Mirroring the implicit expectations placed on privileged students attending elite schools that they would inevitably transition to the most elite universities; the career aspirations of elite students, particularly those from more privileged backgrounds 'are not simply the result of individual preferences but are heavily influenced by organisations and actors inhabiting them' (Binder et al., 2016: 35). For these students, the knowledge that certain jobs are prestigious is constructed and fostered within the broad social life of elite universities. As a result, a 'peer prestige system' develops on elite campuses in which students become aware of the different types of jobs and their rankings based on prestige and earning potential, leading Binder et al. to conclude that 'campus environments, or university fields of power have a large, independent role in the reproduction of social inequality' (2016: 35). The elite university is a specific staging post within a network which enables students to have access to prestigious career pathways, highly selective jobs and recruitment processes (Stevens et al., 2008).

However, this network differentiates along class lines (Weedon and Grusky, 2005), by race (Willie, 2003) and in particular by previous attendance at elite schools. The significance of elite schools is 'often theorised as the institutional starting point of elite trajectories, but their ability to act as such is often strongly mediated by their connections to elite universities' (Reeves et al., 2017: 6). This highlights the connectivity between different elements of education and employment outcomes. The networks between families and institutions and the self-fulfilling processes by which more privileged students succeed throughout their academic careers are reinforced within the recruitment process itself. Rivera identifies 'the way in which elite employers define and evaluate merit in hiring strongly tilts the playing field for the nation's highest-paying jobs toward children from socioeconomic privileged backgrounds' (2015: 25). Students from more privileged backgrounds are likely to both benefit from effective parental educational strategies such as 'concerted cultivation' (Lareau, 2003) and also from the economic advantage of attending elite schools that train and equip students with a particular way of being in the world based on access and acceptance in elite spaces (Lamont et al., 2014). Employers provide elite groups with access to elite jobs and are significant gatekeepers who protect this access only for those from elite schools (Bol and Weeden, 2015). A trajectory emerges in which wealthier families invest economic capital in their children attending elite schools, which in turn smooths their passage to an elite university which provides access and entry into elite employment and privileged positions in the labour market (Kennedy and Power, 2008; Khan, 2012).

The campus is significant because it highlights the local nature in which particular forms of behaviour and particular identifications of value are actively privileged. Despite their global reputations, the identities of successful elite students are shaped within the local settings of their institutions; within their teaching spaces, libraries and college accommodations.

The Performativity of Privilege: 'It's Not Just About Where You Come From, It's About Where You're Going'

The students in our research often identified and described a range of relationships between their past experiences, their current engagement as postgraduate students at elite universities and their expectations for the future. For many students these relationships were foregrounded on characteristics they had developed by the time they reached university but they also tended to look forwards. The accounts they gave of embodied characteristics such as their current knowledge of how elite universities worked, were contextualised in terms of opening up social networks, opportunities and connections that would mostly be valuable in the future. In this sense their *habitus*, their predispositions shaped by a whole range of past experiences integral to structuring their current social world (Bourdieu,

1977) framed their expectations of future successful progression. Given their awareness of the advantages of elite universities and their status as postgraduates it was
unsurprising that they anticipated transitioning towards successful careers. More
significantly, their accounts often provided legitimising narratives of their entitlement to the opportunities that they would accrue from studying at elite universities. As discussed in earlier chapters, these were often narratives in which an
acknowledgement of privileged backgrounds facilitating access to elite universities
was countered by accounts of being rewarded for individual hard work and intelligence. What emerges in our participants' narratives is a shared *doxa*; a sense that
their knowledge of their legitimate occupation of the social space of elite universities can be 'taken for granted' and can be 'seen as self-evident and undisputed,
of which they are the product and of which they reproduce the structures in a
transformed form' (Bourdieu, 1977: 164). Students did not just *take for granted* their
present status of being students at elite universities but also identified their future
success in well-paid, prestigious careers was equally preordained. Significantly in
his accounts of doxa, Bourdieu does not simply identify individuals taking for
granted their rightful positions in society, but rather, portrays the overarching social
norms by which all people tend to understand that they are all situated within their
rightful places in the pecking order (Bourdieu, 1977; Bourdieu and Wacquant,
1992). Inequitable access to elite universities foregrounding successful careers in the
future is normalised not as evidence of inequality but of the natural order of the
social world. Harriet described being aware of the advantages of attending UK1 for
both her undergraduate and postgraduate degree and how it would 'open doors'
for her in the future,

> I know I'm now part of that group [privately educated students] and part of
> that privilege and sense of opportunity that comes with attending [UK1],
> and it will open lots of doors for me that I would not otherwise have. I can
> already see that when I compare my experience to that of my friends who
> went to really good universities but not to [UK1 or UK2]. Their experiences
> have been different to mine. Mine have led me to have more doors just being
> opened for me. It's like people holding open the door and saying, please
> come in, we want you just because I went to [UK1].

In Harriet's account her sense of privilege was directly related to her identification
of personal opportunities; however this was not an understanding of opportunities
that had to be chosen or strived for. Rather, she described opportunities in terms
of people holding open the door; in other words her perception of her social world was
of the ease with which an elite university education translated into an elite career.
That sense of easiness highlights how Harriet's narrative was in effect unchallengeable; she legitimately understood her position because it was shared with other
people around her.

Another student, Jessica (UK1) described how difficult it was 'to get out of
the mould' of an elite university. Jessica had attended UK2 for her undergraduate

studies and wanted a different university experience for her postgraduate studies but felt she could only continue her studies at a comparable institution. She explained how being part of the 'mould' was something that became the norm,

> It almost becomes part of who you are, part of your being, if that makes sense. Once you go to UK2 you can never undo that. That sense of advantage you have. From being served dinners in grand halls to employers literally asking you if you want to work for them and earn a significant amount of money and that's even before you have graduated. Those are the kind of opportunities that become the norm. Once you have had them, you will always expect them and won't have to do the things that other graduates who didn't attend UK2 have to do. Our professors constantly remind us, we are the top 5%, we are the cream, we are the best. And if you're told, it becomes part of you and who you are – and you come to expect the best, *all the time*.

Simon had also studied at two different elite universities for his undergraduate and postgraduate studies. A British student, he graduated from UK1 but decided to continue his postgraduate studies at US2. He described his awareness of the 'prestige' of universities that were only associated with the eliteness of a handful of specific universities including UK1, UK2, US1 and US2. He made the analogy between these universities and English football's 'Premier League',

> It's kind of like football and other divisions that are used to identify the excellent ones from those that are down the pecking order. And that's important if you want to do well, you have to be aware of these things. I came to [US2] because it's the Premier League, it's not division 1 or 2. And I went to [UK1] for the same reason.

As Harriet and Simon's accounts illustrate, students were aware that attending an elite university would enable them to have access to far greater opportunities compared to their peers who had not attended an elite university. This access to future privilege was seen as the norm, something that was expected and something that came naturally. Tom, a Black student studying at US1, was very open about the reasons he had attended an elite student as an undergraduate and as a postgraduate.

> I'm not being shy about this because I know that I wanted to go to a good university, I wanted to ensure that I went to a university which would enable me to be in the top tier for earning potential. Isn't that the only reason you come here to [US1] because you know that it's going to take you far. Coming here is just the beginning, it's where it takes you that matters.

Tom described himself as coming from 'a privileged, educated middle class background' and was clear that his parents had instilled in him a sense of automatically knowing he would end up in a 'great university' which would lead to him being employed in a high earning job.

> I'm not going to be apologetic for my background. It's not my fault I was born into a wealthy family, I have no control over that. I'm not going to waste that privilege by going to a lower tier university. After so many years of hard work and so much debt, I have to make sure I know what the endgame is. It's about being competitive and getting that job that will be the reward for so many years of hard work. I look at my parents and they have a big house, nice cars, and all that. But they have worked hard to get there. They are both lawyers and that's the kind of life I want. Work hard and be super rewarded.

Tom stressed how he could not distance himself from his background and made the point that attributes of his privilege such as his parent's backgrounds, his educated accent and wealth were the same were, 'like the colour of my skin, I cannot pretend it's not there'. For some other students from working-class or less privileged backgrounds the experience of being at an elite university was not as easily managed. This impacted on how they were able to think about their future career paths. Georgina spoke openly about her working-class background and also identified she was less comfortable with processes of using her UK1 experience to help her get a good job,

> I know that this world [UK1] isn't really part of my real world. My family are not from this kind of stock. I was kind of singled out in my school as someone who should go to UK1 because they saw the potential in me. I was supported but am the first in my family – all of my family – to go to university and for it to be UK1 has made my parents and all my family so proud. But I'm here so I have to make the most of it and use it so that I can get a good job and benefit from, otherwise why would I have come here. I have to do what all the other students do who are comfortable being here because it's part of their world. I have to use it like they use it.

The academic journeys of our respondents were as much about where they had come from as well as where they were and their future journeys and transitions into the labour market. All were aware of the advantages they had received from being at an elite university and all were aware the difference the accolade would make to their future careers. As Jessica said,

> Once you have UK2 on your CV – you've made it, you can literally do anything with it. Employers will be bending over backwards to give you a job and employ you and they will pay you a lot of money. All because you have shown you are part of the club. The club of the privileged.

Passing It On

The majority of our participants suggested that they would encourage their own children to apply to elite universities. These included students like Bethany who had struggled to feel comfortable at UK2 because of her working-class background,

> I would send my children to an elite university there are tangible and non-tangible benefits. If you want the best for your children, why wouldn't you? They will make important connections and have access to magnificent networks and huge resources. I would love for my children to have these opportunities. If they can get in, then great.

For more privileged students there was often an expectation that their children would also attend elite universities. These students often appeared to be describing the legitimising processes they had experienced prior to studying at elite universities would naturally be reproduced intergenerationally. They tended to cite both their knowledge of the benefits that accrued from attending elite universities and also the value of their own parents' expectations and strategies to ensure their educational careers materialised. Edward was adamant that he would send his children to an elite university,

> I have seen the value of coming to US2 there are so many doors that are opened to you. Automatically. You don't have to go out and find those opportunities, they are given to you. From kindergarten, I would make it an expectation that I would want my children to strive for the best so they have a goal they can aim for. This is what my parents encouraged me to do. If they work hard, they can achieve those goals.

Similarly, Simon [US2] also was very clear about the benefits and also the role of parents in ensuring the future success of his children,

> I would definitely want my children to go to an Ivy League school. I don't know why you would think otherwise. The magnificent opportunities that are available here at US2 and the access to meeting different professors who are the best is the one thing that we all aspire to. I would encourage my children from an early age to make that their goal just as my parents did for me. If you are raised thinking that is your goal, you will achieve it.

Bart (UK1) stressed the relationship between his own background ensuring his was a natural progression towards study at an elite university and his ambitions for his children to replicate that progression,

> I would encourage my children to come to [UK1]. They would be coming from a background where I have been. My parents and siblings have too. If you

are brought up that way, you don't know any difference and it just becomes the expected thing. You don't think of doing anything different to that.

Zena whose parents were immigrants to the US from Afghanistan and who completed her undergraduate study at a public university was more ambivalent about how she would advise her children in the future. She would support her children whatever decision they made but felt they should also be aware that the long-term career benefits of US1 needed to be balanced against less attractive elements of its culture and ethos,

> There are lots of positive things about coming [US1], the quality of the education is remarkable but it can also have feelings of isolation and alienation. I wouldn't openly encourage them, but if they wanted to go I wouldn't stop them. I would be very open about the possible discrimination they might face. I would be happier if [US1] changed things. Like having mentors who don't come from an elite background, who have the language and culture to appeal to students from different backgrounds and religions.

Conclusions

The long-term benefits of attending elite universities were readily identifiable and attractive to students. These are institutions that open doors to exceptionally prestigious and financially rewarding careers. Our participants all knew that they personally would benefit from their attendance at these universities whatever career path they chose to follow. They also highlighted how their access to elite careers was not something that uniquely emerged because they were successful in applying to study at an elite university. What emerged was a systemic set of social practices in which more privileged actors were constantly being channelled towards successful future careers. Parental background, economic capital, access to elite fee-paying schools were all weighted towards advantaging a particular cohort of more privileged families to ensure their children were successful. This happened through the access these families have to a whole range of capitals. Their wealth provided the economic capital to pay for a private schooling; their social networks delivered the connections and the sense of belonging within an elite social space and underpinning it all was the types of knowledge or cultural capital these families bring to the table. The children of more privileged families were imbued throughout their lives with knowledge that aligned with their families' elite expectations. The final accession to an elite career was understood to be normal and to legitimise their natural progression into privilege. In Bourdieu's analysis this would be understood as a perfect alignment between the access to pre-existing capitals, actors imbued with characteristics and dispositions tailor-made for the spaces of elite social environments. What also emerged in the accounts of less privileged students was the processes by which the legitimisation of privilege is understood more generally than just by those who are most privileged. Less privileged students still identified the value they could derive by accessing prestigious future careers and in consequence their strategies to hold on to these opportunities often flagged a degree of complicity despite their doubts and concerns about the institutions themselves. This mirrors a broader public perception about who attends elite universities and who fills the most prestigious roles in society as a legitimising narrative. The evidence of inequitable outcomes in education often seemingly unchallengeable because there is a generalised acceptance that the beneficiaries of elite university are rightfully reaping the rewards of their hard work and intelligence. This is a narrative that in part is unchallengeable because the visible evidence of its actors' success is all too apparent: The children of privileged families secure elite university places and progress to elite careers.

6

RACE, PRIVILEGE AND INEQUALITY

This chapter will specifically focus on the experiences of students of colour to examine how their race, class and prior experiences had an impact on attending an elite university. The chapter uses critical race theory (CRT) to argue that white elites are produced and reproduced through systemic, structural racism within elite universities. Despite this, new emergent groupings of non-white students within elite universities are identifiable (Hartocollis, 2021; Myers and Bhopal, 2021) and such students contributed to our research. In part, this reflects some institutional responses to increasingly public discourse about the prevalence of racism within elite universities. This includes the persistence of media headlines identifying the low numbers of students of colour attending elite universities in particular Oxford and Cambridge (Quinn, 2018; Rehman, 2019). It also reflects a wider discourse around the whiteness of the Academy (Bhopal, 2018). In 2014, for example, University College London (UCL) hosted a discussion on the theme, *Why Isn't My Professor Black?* (Jahi, 2014), in subsequent years the very small number of professors of colour continues to be identified as a significant indicator of systemic racism within universities (Bhopal, 2022). Racism in UK universities has been framed, very publicly, within anti-racist protest often led by students such as *Why Is My Curriculum White?* and *Rhodes Must Fall* (Andrews, 2020). Universities have responded, notably when faced by short-term moments of crisis such as the emotional surge in support for #BlackLiveMatter following the George Floyd murder in 2020, with their own slogans for action such as *decolonising the curriculum* (Bhambra et al., 2018) and with institutional attempts to remedy the most obvious and pernicious forms of inequality such as 'attainment gaps[1]' in degree awards (UUK/NUS, 2019). Interviewed by *The Independent* in 2021, Professor Kehinde Andrews, the first Black Studies professor in the UK stated, 'I get treated like the uppity negro who should always be grateful for everything and stop complaining' (White, 2021).

DOI: 10.4324/9781003029922-6

What becomes apparent is that racism is not a covert activity with academia. It is readily identifiable within universities own data, within student experience and within the accounts of academics (Myers, 2022). This raises uncomfortable questions about why the calls for change are not acted upon; and, related to this, the role played by new groupings of students of colour in universities. One way to understand the ambiguities inherent in academic racism is through a lens of interest convergence; this might suggest that new groups of non-white elites are primarily fostered within elite universities because it is in the interests of white people to do so. This might happen if the appearance of racist discrimination within elite university admissions became so evidently out of line with public expectations that an institution felt compelled to address the appearance of inequity. By addressing a specific issue (e.g. recruiting more students from minority groups), traditional white interests are seemingly pushed to one side. However, we found evidence that elite universities produce their own hierarchies of eliteness within their institutional practice that allows for the recruitment of students of colour whilst ensuring they sit at the lower end of such hierarchies. These reflect the ongoing struggles for capitals within the university (as discussed in the preceding chapters), which are also determined along lines of race and ethnicity. In this respect elite universities produce a dynamic range of inequality with the production of 'elite haves' (privileged white students) and 'non-elite haves' (students disadvantaged by race/ethnicity and/or social class).

CRT is a particularly useful theoretical tool for understanding the circumstances in which these outcomes materialised in our research for three specific reasons. First, CRT identifies the centrality of race and racism within institutional and social structures; our participants identified racism as a commonplace experience at elite universities but this occasionally felt as though it was lost within the wider accounts of inequality within these institutions. In this respect, CRT provides a useful critical counterpoint to Bourdieu's analysis of patterns of reproduction by identifying racism as a specific context within elite universities that works both independently and in tandem with other processes of inequality. Second, CRT, with the emphasis it places on experience, resonated with research that was drawing upon the lived experiences and accounts of graduate students. This also felt as though it sat comfortably within a Bourdieusian framework for conducting research and the primacy of empirical evidence. Finally, CRT is useful in our context because the theoretical tools it brings to bear upon empirical data such as interest convergence and intersectionality are well-placed to understand the complexities and ambiguities that emerged throughout our data. In the first instance this chapter explores the experiences of racism that students identified whilst attending university, before moving on to consider some of the more ambiguous and problematic consequences that emerged.

The Centrality of Racism Within Elite Universities

All of the students of colour in our sample discussed how they experienced racism in some form whilst studying at elite universities. In many respects this is unsurprising and would reflect wider patterns of student experience at most universities in the UK and the US (Bhopal and Myers, 2022; Bhopal, 2022; Warikoo, 2016). In our study participants recalled direct experiences of racism from their peers and from both academic and non-academic staff; they also provided understandings of how elite structures were themselves implicitly built around racist practice. This was particularly apparent for international students of colour. Hannah was a Malayan student who spoke about the overt racism she experienced as a Muslim woman at UK2. In the first instance she spoke about attitudes towards her appearance and presentation of self, including her accent being mocked by other students and being told she needed to speak more clearly,

> I have had my peers laugh at my accent and I've seen it happen publicly to other students – those who are Indian and Japanese. We are told to speak clearer and told that others cannot understand us. We have to put on a western accent – an American accent so that others can understand us. We are made to feel inferior compared to other students, and this comes across as if we are not as smart as they are.

A number of other students also described being 'openly mocked' or 'laughed at' because of their accent; Hannah's account was notable because she made a direct link between the mockery of her language and how this was interpreted as a sign she was not as intellectually capable as other students. She went on to explain how she was also disadvantaged in her written work because she drew upon scholarship from outside of American and European traditions,

> I wrote an essay on women's experience of oppression in Malaysia and I focussed on the hijab and how oppression works to marginalise women. I used writings that were not on the reading list – they were mainly writers from the Middle East and writers of colour but I was told off. I was marked down and told by my professors that I was biased and I should have used white western feminists to make my arguments. So to me, that said the way you write and what you include is biased towards white scholarship.

What seemed striking was the alignment of student experience and academic demands both actively worked to devalue forms of knowledge Hannah possessed and was creating within her intellectual labour. Individual racisms found a clear privileging within the institutional ethos of the elite university. In this way, racism was playing a significant role in shaping hierarchies in which white students were understood to possess more valuable forms of knowledge. Hannah went on to discuss her experience of micro-aggressions in her relations with other students. Again it was striking how much emphasis she placed on the role of other students to enforce her position as a second-class citizen within the overarching structure of the university,

> Micro aggressions happen all the time here at UK2 – it's known for it – and it can affect your mental health – when you are always afraid you will be singled out in some way because you are different and you do not fit the norm. I also feel those who say they are 'woke' can also take part in those micro aggressions, and if they do it's excused because they think they are 'woke'.

The acceptance of micro-aggressive acts was something that was seen as the norm by many students including Hannah. Speech characteristics associated with speaking in a second language and accents were often cited, as were remarks about clothing. Yvonne, an international Chinese student also studying at UK2, noted that her clothing choices, which she regarded as uncontroversial, generic and typical of the smart clothing she would associate with law students at elite universities in Beijing, seemed to attract attention,

> I get 'looks' if that makes sense. Nothing is said just these looks. If I walk into a room people stare as if I was an alien.

Yvonne noted that it was always impossible to know exactly what other students thought about her but that in conversations with other international students they often identified similar experiences. Yvonne also discussed how precise she was about learning to speak English 'like the English', as a strategy to avoid attracting attention. She explained that she would always spend time each evening understanding colloquialisms or phrases that she was unsure about. Both Yvonne and Hannah spoke about adapting to the elite setting of UK2 because, as Hannah noted,

> I have to adapt to the environment because I have entered it. The environment will not change for me.

They both also noted that their friendship groups and social connections all tended to be framed amongst other students like themselves. Hannah, who had completed her undergraduate studies previously at another elite UK university also discussed her awareness that social class often distinguished the differences between white students. However, she did not feel social class played a significant role in how home students felt about her; the key delineation that made her uncomfortable materialised in the perceptions of her being Muslim, Brown and not white. She also highlighted how more 'progressive' or 'woke' students at both UK2 and her previous university were, whilst apparently engaged in radical campaigns against racism, still seemed uncomfortable in her presence. She felt deeply ambivalent towards an ongoing student campaign protesting racism at UK2 suggesting it was a closed matter for home students rather than a broader representation of all students' concerns. In hindsight, Hannah felt she should not have come to UK2 to study and would not send her children to an elite university in the future,

UK2 has a very high opinion of itself. I knew that if I came here I would get a good job, highly paid. I felt it was obligatory for me, coming here for my family. If I had a choice I would not have come. I had no choice, it was where my family wanted me to go. It sees itself as more superior than anywhere else, and it is more superior because it is UK2. I would not encourage my own children to go to such a university like UK2, even my young siblings didn't go. It is a hostile environment, it's insidious, in your face all the time. You are made to feel you do not belong – from the first moment you are here.

Racism was also identified by home students at elite universities and although often characterised in similar ways to those of international students there were also some differences. Femi spoke about her experiences as a Black British Nigerian. She discussed racism as an everyday occurrence at elite universities that was evidenced in very overt ways and in the form of micro-aggressions. She also made connections between social class and whiteness at elite universities as key determinants of how she would experience racism,

There are different ways in which racism takes place. I was the only Black person on my course and was made to feel different by others, but also felt different myself. When the lecturer said something about Black people everyone would turn and look at me and expect me to be the expert. From the students, it's the posh, white, middle class UK2 boys who dominate – they totally ignore you because you are not like them. They treat you and let you know you are not one of them. They have all been to the same private schools and already know each other before they come to UK2. It really is like an old boy's club.

Racism in Femi's account (as with international students Yvonne and Hannah), materialised in student behaviours which Femi related to the institutional hierarchies that defined the distribution of privilege within UK2. For Femi these were identifiably classed forms of exclusion and in this respect her own feeling of being marginalised because of her race was compounded by her own working-class identity. This awareness of an intersectional classed and raced identity for home students was at odds with the experiences of international students of colour; even Hannah who identified British class distinctions, did not feel these were related to her general experience of racism from British home students. One similarity with international students highlighted by Femi was the need to make adaptations to the elite university environment in order to make her student experience more comfortable. She described how on the one hand she was openly excluded from conversations by mainly though not exclusively 'posh, white, middle class boys', but how she also chose to exclude herself as a protective mechanism,

I also feel as though I exclude myself, I have to for my own sanity. I don't have any white friends here at UK2 – only those who are 'woke'. Only the ones who understand and get that racism is real here. There are also the deniers. Those who simply think it's all in our imagination that we experience racism or that we should get over it and move on.

Many of the students of colour at both UK1 and UK2 mentioned 'woke'. During the time of interviews it was a relatively new term in the UK[2] that was used to describe white individuals who have a clear understanding of race and racism. The term has a longer history of usage in the US, though one that has increasingly become subverted within conservative media as a dismissive label for those on the left. Tellingly, for the international students Yvonne and Hannah, 'woke' was a label for home students who identified as progressive even if this was not borne out by their actions, whilst for Femi the term held a more positive meaning of white allyship. Femi herself also identified distinctions between her experience and those of international students which reflected her identity as both Black British and also working-class British. She went on to talk about how her experience as a Black woman was very different to that of international Black students.

> Here at UK2, they try and portray diversity and inclusion but the Black students here just portray eliteness. 90% of the Black students here are from Nigeria and they went to international private schools, they are not British Nigerian. They come from different backgrounds and are just as privileged as the white, posh privately educated students. UK2 perpetuates privilege not equality and the Black international students perpetuate that privilege.

Femi felt that even though the Black international students were not white, due to their experiences of being from privileged backgrounds characterised as being from the upper middle class, wealthy elites and of having previously attended private schools they were more likely to fit with similar white students. Asked about whether Black international students experienced racism she said,

> I'm not convinced they do. At least not in the same ways as we [working class British Black students] do. They have all the attributes. Like the background, the way they speak and all that familiarity that comes with being privileged so they are part of the group. I think they are more accepted than me because I am working class and come from a single parent family. But then they are not white so will experience that difference in other ways – so I know some of them have spoken about racism from porters and other staff – so it could work in that way.

The differences drawn out between international and home students' experiences of racism suggested that overwhelmingly, students of colour identified that they were devalued within elite universities because of racism towards them. However this happened within a dynamic range of contributory factors that defined different types of racisms. Being Black and British entailed being subjected to a different form of racism to that of being Brown and Malaysian; in both cases however the impact of race and racism remained central to how students felt they were positioned within institutional hierarchies.

The complexities of these processes were further demonstrated in the account of another international student Anya studying at UK1. Anya was a US citizen from a family of Indian heritage, she was born and grew up in the US and attended an elite Ivy League university before moving to the UK for postgraduate study. She spoke about her changing experience and growing awareness of racism since beginning her studies at elite universities on both sides of the Atlantic,

> I never thought of myself as an outsider until I went to an elite university. After Trump's election, this had real repercussions for race relations in the US. You could see how toxic all the different environments became, even those you thought would never be part of that, the universities and inclusive spaces. I felt I had to re-evaluate my identity, who I was and what I stood for. It was a rude shock that made us think of how we belonged.

Nema (US1) also echoed Anya's comments that the election of Donald Trump as President had changed the nature and perception of racism dramatically both in society as a whole, but also within the university context.

> In the last couple of years to be a person of colour at US1 has been fraught and there have been tensions and this has only escalated with the politics we now stand for in this country. Police brutality is one thing that has deteriorated in all areas and across all campuses.

For Anya, moving to the UK was a means of adapting to both an uncomfortable political climate in the US and also her concerns about the impact this was having on her university experience. She outlined how her experience of growing up in the US, she was from an affluent family and attended exclusive private schools, had not prepared her for the racism she encountered in an elite US university. She noted this was the first time she felt her Indian heritage seemed to be called into question, 'Bluntly speaking, at [Ivy League university] I found I was Indian not American'. As a consequence, when Anya made the decision to continue with postgraduate studies to fulfil her ambitions of becoming an academic these experiences both informed her choice of institution and also her perceptions of UK1.

> There is an inherent, social and symbolic value of being at UK1. It is a recognised name and makes people sit up and listen. If you are those people who are relevant from a social standpoint then you have access to certain things. You may come from one of those wealthy Indian families who can make a significant financial contribution to the university. You are seen as adding to the richness of the intellectual world that exists here at UK1. If

you don't come from that kind of family you may experience some kind of discrimination.

It was apparent that Anya was acutely aware that she was positioned in a very privileged position. As a very wealthy American student her transition to an elite university demonstrated her ability to draw upon her own easy access to capitals and mobility. Under other circumstances it is likely she might have remained in the US as a graduate student. Despite her own privileged background and despite her recognition that she could find a relatively easy 'fit' amongst the elites at UK1, she still identified racism as a central tenet of elite universities in both the UK and the US. Her understanding that her affluent Indian background might signal some of the determining factors of that 'fit' was also central to Anya's observation of racism within UK1. She identified that those students who were from working class and less affluent backgrounds were disadvantaged.

> If you have some students who are not white but are also working class and maybe not so middle class, they are the ones who experience more because of that difference. And that difference is then related to race and so they are immediately seen as being not as good, not as clever. They don't have the means to compensate for their class.

The 'means' in Anya's sense was the mix of economic and social capital that she understood she brought to bear whilst studying at UK1.

Stuart who was from a Latino background and studying at US2 spoke about his own experiences of racism. In particular he identified both the overarching centrality of racism to the experience of attending an elite university but also the individual ways in which that emerged because of his difference,

> As a Latino, the first in my family to go to university, I am seen as being different. I think I am often seen as an indifferent student. No one thinks I am a problem but no one is that interested. I am different because I am not white and I am different because I am not Black. Coming here to US2 which is one of the best universities in the world has made me realise how my background has a big effect on how people see me. There are not many Latinas here and so I am seen as different to [US2 students]. I am not seen as threatening. I know some of the Black male students are seen as threatening by other students and by the faculty.

Stuart commented on the lack of Latino representation at both the student and staff levels. He felt that Latinos were often left behind when issues of race were being addressed because greater emphasis was placed on the experience of Black students. At the same time, he identified a tendency in which the university seemed to assume that Latino experiences and Black experiences simply overlapped,

It is hard to fit in when you are given this message. There are ways we are different from the Black students. Our migration stories are very different and how we are treated is different. And that matters.

Stuart's account highlighted many of the key ambiguities about race in elite universities. On the one hand, students of colour are seemingly identified as a single body differentiated by their race or ethnicity. They consequently share a number of defining experiences including the experience of racism as a routine feature of their student experience. However within that narrative it was also clear that students faced very different types of racism that could be calibrated by their country of origin, religious affiliation, relative affluence and class status; as well as by individual traits, often associated with these, such as accent or choice of clothing. These variables created a dynamic economy in which race and ethnicity were overwhelmingly devaluing the worth of students of colour within the elite university but also positioning different groups and individuals in relation to each other based on the racist perception of markers, traits and other characteristics by the dominant white university population. This economy of racist delineations of status seeming to mirror and often intersect with the competition for capitals that would inform a Bourdieusian perspective of class fractions. We identified a hierarchy of oppression in the experiences of students of colour at elite universities in which the disadvantage of race intersects with class identity. Some students of colour from some middle-class, wealthy backgrounds were able to be more comfortable in the elite space of the university. This largely rests upon their prior knowledge and experience of attending an elite university and private schools and access to capitals allied with a white understanding of that status. For students who are not from American or European backgrounds, what materialised was a far less comfortable engagement with the elite space. Amongst the range of determining factors about belonging there was much evidence to show international students were freighted with a particular racist understanding of their foreignness; being both not white and not from the US or the UK they seemed unable to deploy the same traction that Anya identified as a wealthy, American student with an Indian heritage. The value of students within elite universities was therefore related to their race and ethnicity and to their social class and also to the specific perceptions of those features by other individuals and by the institution.

Navigating the Elite Space

Students of colour often contextualised their awareness of inequitable hierarchies within elite universities in terms of how they navigated its spaces. In some respects, their experiences reflected those of their white peers but they also described disparities in their experience specific to their ethnicity. Those from traditional middle-class backgrounds (based on their parents' occupations) and those whose undergraduate study was at an elite university, spoke of prior experiences that influenced their understanding of how to behave and act within an elite university. Those students who were not from traditional middle-class backgrounds and for whom this was their first experience of an elite university often found it harder to adjust. One such student was Ria who described her mixed heritage background. Her father was Indian and her mother was white British. Her dad was a grocer and her mother worked in a school with excluded children. She did not consider herself privileged in any way. Her parents struggled financially and worked hard to send her to university and then financially supported her to attend UK1 for her postgraduate degree.

> For my undergraduate degree I didn't attend an elite university like this one, but I did attend a very good university. It was a shock when I came here, and I knew it would be markedly different but it was on a different scale. As soon as I arrived I knew I would have to think about how I stood out in front of all these other white students who seemed to be feeling very comfortable in their own skin – and in the environment.

Ria spoke about how she immediately felt like she had to change her behaviour to fit in with her peers who were seemed better suited to the social space of UK1,

> I was a bit worried when I saw the other students, they just seemed to know the ropes. They knew when to speak and when not to, they knew what to say, and they knew who to speak to. It was almost as though they were marking out their territory. Saying to the academics, "this is me, remember me and know who I am". I didn't get it at first. It was totally different at [UK university]. I didn't know how it worked but then I realised I had to do it.
> Interviewer: So what did that mean, what did you do?
> Well, it meant I had to ensure that people knew who I was and what I was doing. I realised afterwards that being here meant I had to be noticed for future jobs and future opportunities. I had to speak to as many people as possible, but to be honest it was difficult for me and it didn't help me in the end anyway. Because the opportunities always went to the same people. White students. Very posh ones.

Nema, a Black student at US1, also spoke about similar processes of learning to navigate the university spaces. She came from a working-class, single-parent family brought up by her mother, who was a teacher in a public school in the US. Nema's previous experience included attending an elite university for her undergraduate degree but still felt a sense of having to fit in at US1, though admittedly she did not struggle with this process.

> As an undergraduate I was fortunate enough to earn a scholarship because I was from an under privileged background. My mum is on her own and works three jobs to look after the four of us. I have three other siblings.

Going to [US University] it was initially a shock but I learnt different ways of behaving, which in a way come naturally to be me now. I know I am different to my peers. Most of them seem to be very rich and they have followed in their parents and siblings footsteps, so this is a natural progression for them. I know I have to be able to part of the crowd to get on but I also know that sometimes that makes me feel uncomfortable because I'm not really part of the crowd. I pretend to be.

Being 'part of the crowd' was one of the ways that Nema navigated the space of the elite university. She admitted that all her friends were very different to her and she often changed her own behaviour when she was with them. In particular she described being careful not to appear 'too political' in conversations that touched upon race,

I have to be mindful sometimes of myself. I have to check myself because I don't want to keep going on about issues that I think are going to annoy or upset my peers. So we have lots of conversations at the moment about affirmative action and how that works and who it benefits. I try not to say too much because then I will be seen as the outsider and all I want to do is to make sure I fit in and do what I need to do to get through the course. So it's sometimes a different person you will see.

On the other hand, both of Edward's (Black US2) parents were professionals. His father was a lawyer and his mother a doctor. Edward described how coming from an affluent background rather than his race was most relevant to his experience of being a student. Class and wealth determined where he had come from and where he was going.

I went to an elite university before coming here and both my brothers went to [elite university in the US]. I am fortunate that both my parents also went to very good universities and they have ensured that this is translated to us. I feel quite comfortable in these environments because I have in some ways been here before. I know what these universities are like and I feel comfortable here. My parents have taught me that I am an equal. I am just as intelligent as my peers and I can do just as good as them if not better. I know I have had lots of advantages based on my background but I also know that I have to work hard to achieve a positive outcome.

Edward was conscious of the lack of students of colour at elite universities, but he attributed this to a competitive culture in higher education, rather than inequalities based on race and class.

There are inequalities in the education system but we can't keep blaming it all on the systems and the practices. We also have to look at the individual to see what they are doing. Success comes from hard work and being the best at what you do. And that takes a lot of hard work. Sometimes students of colour forget that and ignore their own failings and blame the system.

Whilst on the one hand, Edward was aware of his own advantageous background, he attributed his own success to hard work. He acknowledged that his middle-class, privileged background in many ways had shielded him from aspects of racism that other students, from less privileged and working-class backgrounds faced. Edward did not doubt that racism was a significant issue, just that it was less impactful on his experience at US2 because of his background,

> I am aware that racism is a thing. It's real and we read about it all the time in the media. But if you look at how that works, it is usually those Black families who haven't had the opportunities that I may have had. They may have experienced poverty, through no fault of their own and that has had an impact on their own lives.

Edward's account of his relative comfort attending US2 was largely framed within the expectations of affluent students who understood their family background positioned them very effectively to access elite universities but tempered this within accounts of their own intelligence and hard work. In his account of race and racism in the university Edward adopted a colour-blind approach. Although the wider prevalence of racism was acknowledged, in the elite university space it became less significant. If anything he attributed race in his own narrative to being a significant positive element of his upbringing related to his family imbuing him with pride about his background and never feeling inferior because of his race. At the same time he associated students from less privileged backgrounds as both lacking his opportunities and also attributing blame to failings in the system.

Deena (UK2) was an international student from India who, like Edward, was also from an affluent, privileged background. Both her parents went to university in India and she had attended an elite university in the US for her undergraduate degree. Unlike Edward her previous experience of affluence and attending another elite university did not translate so easily into feeling comfortable at UK2. She identified being ill at ease with the university in respect of her ethnic identity and her peer's class identity,

> There is a certain privilege that comes when you attend a university like [UK2]. This experience is odd to me because class is hidden in the US. Here it's not, it's in the open, it's everywhere you go. It's there in all sorts of ways and you cannot hide from it or get away from it. The first thing is being served 3 course meals in tuxedos. That is something that is very alien to me. Then it's having access to castle buildings and porters and these dinners. It makes me feel uncomfortable, it makes me feel it's not me. As a whole, I don't think I fit in and I find myself being isolated because of this. I'm a

foreigner because I don't come from here and I'm an alien because I don't belong in an Ivory Tower.

Deena's experience of class hierarchies at UK2 was that they were alien and unexpected; in contrast to her time at a US elite university they were also far more visible. Deena went on to explain how this affected how she navigated the space of UK2,

> I tend to do my own thing, hibernate sometimes in my room. It makes me feel safe and I can relax. I've had weird encounters with people here, my own peers who go to all these society functions, but that's just not me. I'm rarely invited, but if I am I say I am busy. I excuse myself.

Deena identified that her self-exclusion from prominent societies and attending events would make a difference in terms of her outcomes from attending an elite university. In particular the value of social capital that would accrue by making better connections and joining networks was lessened. She described how despite this, her withdrawal from the wider social life of the university was a coping mechanism which ensured she stayed 'authentic'.

> I don't want to lose sight of who I am. I want to ensure I stay authentic to myself. I feel I have experienced a bizarre section of the universe in an intimate way but one that is so divorced from everyday reality. For me the class differences are so overt, and this is done intentionally. It's done so that you are made to feel from the very first moment you come here that this is your place now. It's a place of upper class privilege.

For some students, the experience of racism in their university was made more problematic because they found the institutional structures were unwilling to acknowledge that racism was a problem. Nema discussed how talking about racism, including talking about her own experiences of racism, was closed down by the US1 institutional culture,

> It [racism] has been an issue for me, it has affected me and made me feel that there is a lot of pressure from all quarters. There is the notion that at US1 it's not happening and you wouldn't really talk about it if it is. I wouldn't particularly go to my advisor and tell her I was experiencing racism. Actually, there is no one on the faculty I would speak to about racism unless it was longstanding and happening every day. US1 doesn't feel like a space where you can complain, if you do complain you are seen as weak and unprepared. People say that it's hard, but academia is hard. If you did complain, it would not be viewed as positive by the faculty and it would probably affect if you were employed here in the future. US1 like to think they are virtuous and moral in these things. They would want to take the higher ground and not

be seen as guilty. They would not want their own reputation to be damaged because they are US1, the best university in the world.

Nema made the point she primarily sought support from her friendship networks and that these were all amongst other students of colour. In this respect she mirrored Femi's account of adapting to her environment by restricting her friendships to other students of colour and a handful of 'woke' white students.

> My closest friends are all people of colour, they are my coping mechanism. I can speak to them about anything. About racism and how it works on campus. US1 is not really seen as a place for us students of colour. So I have had to actively seek out spaces where there are students of colour. I don't socialise on campus like my classmates do, I actively seek out organisations which are directed towards students of colour. We do activities that I would describe as being bonding activities. We have a closeness we share based on our oppression.

Nema went on to describe how academics at US1 often dismissed discussions about racism on campus. She described a senior member of faculty's 'insensitivity' when students asked for racist incidents on campus be addressed by the university. According to Nema, despite a number of students raising the same issue the faculty member was unwilling to act to address instances of racism. Nema associated the lack of action with an overriding sense that US1 somehow did not have to mobilise itself to address racism because of its institutional status,

> I think it all comes down to the power that US1 has not just here in the States but in the world. US1 is US1, ultimately it is a fundamentally conservative place, it's not radical at all. It's slow to change its ways because there is no incentive to change, it doesn't have to because it's US1. So the attitude is, if it doesn't work for you, then it's your problem. We have to work so hard as students to raise these issues [racism], to get them out in the open – but ultimately I feel US1 doesn't have to deal with them. They will always be US1 and students will always want to come here.

Students' engagement with their institution and other peers was differently framed by a range of prior experiences determined by race and class. It was noticeable that sharp intersectional distinctions emerged depending on individual student identities and institutional characteristics. Consequently the relatively affluent and privileged backgrounds of Edward and Deena resulted in very different experiences in the US and UK institutions. Whilst Edward concluded that race was not a significant issue at US2 this was not a widely shared view amongst our participants (and was slightly contradicted in Edward's own account of less privileged Black students). In many respects the accounts of Ria, Nema, Edward and Deena demonstrated the significance of the differing intersectional experiences of students of colour at elite universities. Class and pre-existing privilege clearly differentiated students accounts. Deena's background as in international student from India had a specific recalibrating affect on her privilege in the setting of a UK elite university (one that was different to her previous experience in a US university). All these students identified the significance of race and racism within wider social discourse in addition to student life. Their perception of race and racism was identified as a distinct calibrating factor of their own status within university hierarchies.

Intersectional Identities: The Dynamic Range of Racism in Elite Universities

In the previous chapters we discuss the role played around class identities and access to affluence and privilege. In many respects the inequalities that these factors introduce are complex, but still easier to map than those that result as a result of students' race or ethnicity. Bourdieu's tools of habitus, capitals and field provide an effective means of unpacking students' access to pre-existing privilege and resources that can align with the institutional ethos of an elite university. Our discussions with students of colour highlighted that their personal experience and their observation of their peers' experience were also framed by these same conditions. They also described how race and racism impacted upon those experiences generally detrimentally. However, what became apparent was the diversity of racisms that was identified and its relationship with a range of personal attributes. Students identified clear distinctions between racism encountered by home students and that by international students; there were also distinctions between international students, for example between American students of Indian heritage studying in the UK and Indian students from India. In addition students highlighted the impact of changing political conditions at home and their different experiences of engaging with white 'woke' students. What emerged was both the evidence of the centrality of racism within the field of elite universities as a normal, and largely taken-for-granted state of affairs; but also that this was a fragmented experiences. Different students were affected differently and faced different consequences. In this sense, the overarching hierarchies determined by access to capitals and habitus were further calibrated by a range of racisms. There was a seeming capriciousness about the impact and experience of different types of racism; unlike accounts of class attributes, race seemed less clearly defined in the accounts of students. The scale of impact racism might have on different students was both described differently by different students depending on their personal circumstances and institution. It was also accounted for differently by students of colour about each other with some home students suggesting racism was less significant for rich international students, for example (or alternatively international students attributing greater significance to home students' class attributes). One consequence was that it often appeared as though the significance of racism was fractured within the class hierarchies of elite universities. It was not hidden (racism was consistently identified), but it was less well-defined as a consistent structural condition or pattern of behaviours.

Notes

1   'Attainment gaps' refers to the statistically evidenced gap in awards of degrees given to white students compared to other students with similar prior measures of achievement. Across all the UK universities, students of colour are 10.8% less likely to be awarded a first or 2:1 degree than comparable white students (AdvanceHE, 2021).
2   The term 'woke' was included for the first time in the 2017 edition of the Oxford English Dictionary (OED) (OED, 2017).

7

GLOBAL BRANDS AND THE FIELD OF ELITE UNIVERSITIES

Brands

Although readily identifiable, brands are difficult to define or quantify. In particular they are difficult to value and are literally included amongst an organisation's 'intangible assets' (Aaker, 1991). As an 'intangible' form of capital on corporate or institutional balance sheets their measurement by accountants is, 'a conceptual practice – it is a form of attribution, recognition and figuring out' that 'resists accounting legibility' (van Eekelen, 2015: 456). The graduate students who participated in this research, however, often identified the 'brand' of their elite university as something more tangible and recognisably signifying value.

> From my room I can see two car parks and any given day they are full of coaches. That's coachloads of tourists who don't come here to study but to buy into the brand. The big UK1. You can't move for tourists from England. America. China. Japan wherever. All over the world. The name and the associations that are welded to it are overwhelming.
>
> *(Alexandra, UK1)*

This awareness of brands is unsurprising given their ubiquity within commercial and non-commercial economies. Their use as a means of identifying information about an object's origin and quality can be traced back at least 4,000 years to the Indus Valley, where seals were used as a mark of provenance and quality (Moore and Reid, 2008). The characteristics of brands have changed over time; noticeably so in the twentieth century becoming less concerned about conveying informational characteristics and more concerned to portray images associated with power and value and increasingly brand personality (Aaker, 1991; Moor, 2007; Murphy, 1990). This is often achieved by positioning brands as the drivers of shared,

DOI: 10.4324/9781003029922-7

collective experiences in which the investment of individual consumers is within the brand itself, rather than a branded good (Hart, 1998; Murphy, 1998).

One consequence of shifts in brand positioning is that valuation of the brand also changes. The transformation of brands in late modernity is characterised by their emergence as signs that only have meaning in the context of themselves (Baudrillard, 1993); their valuation consequently reflects the logic of brands producing their own measures of value. The brand of *Nike,* for example ceases to be the brand of a shoe or multiple shoes, it is not even the brand of a footwear manufacturing company. *Nike* becomes a multiple-functioning range of brands (including *NikeLab, Jordan, ACG*[1] and *Nike Pro*), that reinforce each other's meanings and produce knowledge about the brand, that is understood universally. In this respect the brand is subsumed within its own organic structure; consuming the brand is irrevocably aligned with consuming the knowledge the brand produces. The knowledge produced by *Nike* is brand-led knowledge, its *NSRL*[2] release, for example is, 'an in-depth study of cold-weather running that resulted in ahead-of-their-time apparel solutions' (NikeLab, 2021). Whilst the added value a brand such as *Nike* confers on a pair of running shoes was always a nebulous accounting calculation; the value of consumer investment in 'ahead-of-their-time apparel' has even less comparable context on which to assign value. Whilst the calculation of value that emerges in the relationship between the consumer, the product and the brand is a problematic equation to solve or quantify; it is a relationship that works on the recognition of the brand as meaningful. Many students cited the immediate recognisability of their elite university brand, not just in terms of Alexandra's comments about tourists visiting the campus to buy branded goods but also in terms of the field of higher education,

> My ambition right now is to clear this hurdle [PhD] and then work towards tenure. In a university like US1. The name is really significant. Every time I hear names like Harvard, Yale, Oxford they are loaded with credibility. No one questions my credibility right now because I'm at US1 and in the future I want that to carry on.
>
> *(Tom, US1)*

And when asked to elaborate on why his credibility went was unquestioned,

> Every academic I meet immediately knows US1. It does not need an expla-nation. For me that is really helpful. Its more than validation of the work being good. The name of US1 is taken for granted as absolute quality. What I am doing now is the leverage for working here in the future and never having to begin a conversation by justifying my position. The name avoids any doubt.

Tom was describing the recognisability the brand of US1 imposed on his aca-demic authority that mirrors the recognisability Bourdieu identifies as significant to many forms of cultural capital (1986; 1989). The accounts of Alexandra and Tom suggested knowledge about the elite university brand was imbued with different understandings of value by different actors but that the overarching authority of the brand name was always unquestioned. In the institutional understandings of US1 and other elite university brands, the authority they imbue in forms of knowledge produced by their institutions is exponentially valuable because it is the cultural capital that legitimises academic knowledge globally. Tom's description that he did not have to explain or justify his academic authority indicates that whilst all universities have brand identities, elite universities have brand identities that provide the ultimate legitimacy of whose value counts the most.

For universities, knowledge has a range of meanings and values. There is the 'pure' knowledge produced by research work and then there is knowledge about the production of that knowledge. One of the key intersections between knowledge produced and knowledge deployed as brand knowledge by universities is evident in the role played by elite universities. By nature of their 'eliteness' they are positioned to assess the value of knowledge production. By doing so, they have a potential means of overcoming the accounting difficulties identified by van Eekelen (2015); in effect their privileged position allows them to verify the greater value of knowledge they produce in comparison to that emerging from less elite universities. Their brand is both a feudal seal of provenance and quality; and, at the same time, it is much more. The brands of Oxford and Cambridge, Harvard and MIT are processing and structuring how knowledge is produced, valued and consumed.

Working Brands

It is too simplistic to suggest university brands, those of both elite and non-elite institutions, have become increasingly designed to promote an image of the university above and beyond providing simple information about its function, as a direct consequence of increasingly marketised higher education economies. However, for many universities competing to recruit students the development of a brand identity within their marketing strategies is undisputed. Ali-Choudhury et al. (2009) identify significant changes to British university branding since the 1960s, arguing the nineteenth-century idealism of universities as places, 'for liberal education and the teaching of universal knowledge' (Newman, 1889: 5) have been radically displaced by policy promoting commercialisation and commodification of the higher education economy. Interviewing Marketing Directors at 25 British universities Ali-Choudhury et al. (2009) chose not to conduct interviews at elite universities such as Oxford, Cambridge or the LSE because,

> they do not have to compete for students in the same ways as the other members of the sample. These internationally renowned institutions are greatly oversubscribed, impose entry requirements over and above those demanded by other universities, do not have to advertise in order to attract students and recruit most of their domestic intakes from a narrow section of the

community. As such, they serve markets that differ in many crucial respects from those served by the rest of the UK higher education system (2009: 16).

This hints at a broader explanation for how and why elite university brands work differently to other institutions. Looking to select rather than recruit students, elite university brands often appear to perform a restrictive role, keeping the masses out rather than drawing them in. At first glance the brand might appear to be non-commercially orientated in this context; designed to produce types of knowledge that are understood and attractive to smaller rather than larger cohorts of students. Its value driven by a more complex dynamic than that facing other universities in which student numbers are a more central component of income generation.

The intangibility of brand value on balance sheets reflects the complexity of its capital value determined by its relational association with other capitals (e.g. economic or social capital) and its active role within economies. Despite the apparent nebulous nature of brands, characteristics of their fluctuating, ill-defined relationship to wider social practice are mirrored throughout marketing, accountancy and sociological accounts. Brands work as social instruments, they are both affected by and affective upon, social life.

Placing a specific value on the brand is useful for accountancy purposes identifying corporate values at one moment in time (such as the calculation of annual profit and loss at the year-end), but ignores the temporal flux in value and significance that inevitably transpire from the brands' role within economies. Bourdieu identifies the capital value of commercial brands as symbolic capital that,

> resides in the mastery of symbolic resources based on knowledge and recognition, such as "goodwill investment", "brand loyalty", etc.; as a power which functions as a form of credit, it presupposes the trust or belief of those upon whom it bears because they are disposed to grant it credence.
>
> *(Bourdieu, 2005: 195)*

This very sociological account of value aligns with a marketing strategy analysis that identifies five indicators of value,

> One is based on the price premium that the name can support. The second is the impact of the name on customer preference. The third looks at replacement value of the brand. The fourth is based on stock price. The fifth focuses on the earning power of a brand.
>
> *(Aaker, 1991: 22)*

Sociological, marketing and accountancy definitions of brands all identify the relational work brands deliver within economies; brands affect other forms of capital. From a commercial perspective the focus of interest is on economic performance; but this is a narrow perspective, and in our discussion of university brands there is a particular interest in how brands affect other forms of capital such as cultural capital and social capital. Whilst the assumption that brands are 'robust and capable of surviving adversity' (Hart, 1998: 4) reflects their inherent value, there are multiple accounts of brands sabotaged through lack of care or catastrophic management.

Protecting the Brand

Protecting the brand to protect an institution's position and status includes the 'conservation or transformation of the "exchange rate" between different kinds of capital and, along the same lines, control of the bureaucratic instances which are in a position to modify the exchange rate through administrative measures' (Bourdieu, 1998b: 34). The notion of an 'exchange rate' between different brand capital and economic capital underpins the calculations accountants make to assign value. In this respect, just as sociological and marketing analyses of brand bear striking similarities; so too sociological and accounting practice overlap. For commercial concerns brands relational positioning can mean they decline due to movement and change within other forms of capital; the growth in online streaming technology, for example seeing the rapid decline of 'Blockbuster' and rapid ascendancy of 'Netflix'. Marketing directors at non-elite universities are wise to plan for and adapt their brands in relation to their marketing strategies which are likely to be more subject to the fluctuations of demographics, political and social change. Educational policy calling for an increase in student numbers requires new forms of marketing of the attractions of universities, their campuses and modules to a new cohort of students; but it is also likely to require the brand to adapt. The brand being the medium through which the universities new role is understood. In the past a university branded on the virtues of being small, local and friendly may wish to slightly refocus as local, friendly and with great links to a major city. For selective institutions, and elite universities in particular such adaptations are unnecessary and probably counter-productive unless faced by a different type of challenge. A broadening of interest in structural inequalities, for example might require some elite universities to rethink how they present themselves publicly but within the existing brand rather than repositioning themselves. In their struggles to maintain brand ascendancy, elite universities have a particularly potent lever to protect and manipulate the exchange rates affecting their value; they are in effect positioned as *producers of knowledge*. In this role they can produce the knowledge that legitimises their own brand ascendancy.

The knowledge produced by universities in this sense is a very specific type of knowledge different to *pure* knowledge, a mathematical theorem, for example, which Stiglitz identifies as a 'global public good' (1999: 4). Whilst elite universities are active in sharing pure mathematical theories and understandings of their significance, they also produce knowledge that situates its significance within closed, private means of production or as cultural capital (Bourdieu, 1984). This is knowledge framed within local institutional production by academics from the institution and shared more exclusively with its students. The value of this capital is inevitably not distributed evenly; it is capital that is up for grabs. It is capital that is being competed for on a continual basis by individual actors whose success is determined by a range of relational factors including their own prior access to capitals, their individual characteristics and how these align with the rules of the field. The brand in this context has a capital value, that is both competed for and consumed by the many actors engaged in university life; but also, a capital value that is being produced. In this sense the brand is an endlessly emergent feature of the social life of universities. It is also a feature that emerges in relation to specific imbalances of cultural capital. Bourdieu describes actors who have successfully acquired educational forms of cultural capital and who have also inherited (through family backgrounds) high forms of cultural capital as enjoying a 'dual form of cultural nobility, the self-assurance of legitimate membership and the ease given by familiarity' (1984: 74). The brand knowledge of elite universities works to restrict access to the brand's knowledge both by being a restrictive bar on recruitment and also by its alignment of characteristics necessary to deploy the brand.

Marginson (2007) unpacks the private:public nature of global education 'goods' arguing they are best understood in terms of the characteristics of their production rather than by a narrow account of their legal ownership. So, a university producing knowledge may be a public institution, but if access to and engagement with the university is restricted (by high tuition fees or a biased selection process for example), this would be the characteristics of production of 'private' goods. Consequently, as national educational policy changes so too the private/public characteristics of educational provision change. If university education is increasingly marketised within neoliberal economies, then the types of education delivered become more a 'private' good even if ostensibly they are delivered as state education.

Marginson (2007) suggests the status that accrues from higher education is better understood as 'positional goods', rather than in Bourdieu's terms as *cultural capital* or in economic terms as *human capital*. He argues,

> Institutions allocate scarce places that provide students selected into those places, and/or able to purchase those places, with immediate prestige, and with the opportunity post-graduation to secure superior incomes, social status and the "social capital" derived from student networking. The positional good is then enfolded in the degree certificate, a portable currency of the claim to social position.
>
> *(Marginson, 2007: 36)*

Positional goods are distinguished from cultural capital on the basis their valuation is too intrinsic to individual *habitus* and does not take enough account of social demand; but this sounds like an argument in which education is expected to function as a free-market economy. Bourdieu's account would presume a shaping relationship between the social and the individual; one that might be observed in the status imbued into the bodies of elite university agents. Marginson's (2007) corrective to the economists position is stronger; that too much emphasis is placed on a value associated with financial rewards. The brands of elite universities establish the value of knowledge produced within their institutions and bestowed upon their academic staff, students and alumni. Such knowledge holds a value in excess of its pure knowledge value, which can be understood as a positional private good or as cultural capital. In this sense the understanding of the same mathematical theorem by a graduate of the University of Oxford and a graduate of Oxford Brookes University[3] is not distinguished solely by their individual ability or knowledge; but rather by their access to institutional value and the exchange rates for cultural capital produced by their institution. The alignment of greater and lesser status based on institutional affiliation reflects the social calculation of value identified by Tom when describing the unassailable status of his university brand.

Lury (2004) suggests brands operate in a similar fashion to the role of 'money' in Simmel's (1978) account of social life, by calibrating the relational value of objects; though she distinguishes Simmel's money working as the 'means' whilst brands are 'a medium' (Lury, 2004: 4). As arbiters and producers of knowledge, global elite universities exert significant sway through their brand names as a medium for understanding, measuring or calibrating cultural capital. The ability for elite universities to legitimise knowledge is a valuable currency in the competition for resources institutionally in terms of reputation, research funding and increased student numbers; and also individually, in terms of career prospects.

Elite University Brands

Elite university brands are often characterised by a mixture of universities' local attributes (including institutional histories and ethos), national and global identities. This reflects their increasing competition in economies in which the 'global and the local do not exist as cultural polarities but as combined and mutually implicating principles' (Beck, 2002: 17). The entanglement of the local and global in brands, finds a corollary in Bourdieu's concept of 'field'; the relational structures that bind institutions and their agents in continuous competition for resources and power or 'capitals' (Bourdieu and Wacquant, 1992). A university is one example of a local 'field' in which academics, students, departments and faculties, compete for position and resources. The broader national 'field' of higher education is the space in which universities compete with each other (Bourdieu, 1988). For elite universities, the global economies in which they compete can also be conceived as a specific 'field'; one in which institutionally and individually its agents deploy its brand as a form of capital. The university brand encompasses economic, cultural and social capitals in a collision of relational and transactional processes that resonates with Lury's account of brands as 'a kind of privately owned currency' (2004: 138) in which the circulation of dominant ideas organises the economy.

The most successful global brands imbued with the most value represent a very small tranche of instantaneously recognisable narratives about commercial concerns, goods or other services. *Apple, Chanel, NATO, POTUS* are recognisably cut from a different cloth to other ostensibly elite brands whose value is tempered by status and geography: Mozilla's *Firefox* is a successful and respected brand but in a lesser league to Google's *Chrome*; *John Lewis* and *Waitrose* are well-respected UK distributors of a range of goods and services online and in the high street but their brand identity is deep in the shadow of *Amazon*.

As discussed in Chapters 1 and 2 there are some broad definitions of what identifies an elite university. In the UK membership of the Russell Group, for example or internationally universities placed in the top 100 of the *QS World Rankings*. However, these overarching categories although identifying excellent universities with long-standing reputations for being at the forefront of knowledge production, do not also distinguish the impact of brand value held by a small number of institutions. Within the Russell Group the global brands of Oxford, Cambridge, LSE or Imperial are recognisably in a different league to Sheffield, Southampton or Exeter. The 100 World Universities includes Harvard, Stanford, MIT and Yale but also Tübingen, Glasgow and RWTH Aachen. The brand name of some elite universities indicates a particular form of value that differentiates them not just from all other universities but also from broader definitions of the best universities in the world.

Drawing on Bourdieu's (1993a) analysis of educational fields, Marginson (2008) identifies a polarity between an 'elite subfield of restricted production, and the subfield of large-scale mass production tending towards commercial production' (2008: 305). Marginson argues this translates into the global bloc of elite universities dubbed the 'Global Super-League' by *The Economist* (2005). What is striking is how readily identifiable members of *The Economist's* super-league are; their limited numbers; their American-Anglo locations; and the consistency of their ascendancy (ten years on, or 50 years previously we would still identify the same cohort). The super-league consists entirely of Ivy League, Oxbridge and a small number of immediately recognisable, prestigious universities including a handful of Russell Group institutions.[4] Their collective nomenclatures are instantly recognisable global brands: Oxford or Harvard, the LSE or MIT.

Elite University Brands and Global Reach

Kornberger (2015) describes the Harvard University brand functioning 'as a resource for individual identity and as medium for collective identification' (2015: 109); in this sense it has a 'currency' (Lury, 2004) in shaping the social world. Such 'currency' includes the production and consumption of knowledge or cultural capital by elite universities; freighted with high levels of branded value characterised by its recognisable authority when legitimising political and social orthodoxies (Bourdieu and Wacquant, 1992). For elite universities in particular, engagement and competition within global economies have long been a standard practice. One that has been fostered by the ascendancy of neoliberal economies associated with greater private investment within traditionally state-run education practices, simultaneously matched by increasingly market-driven practice in the state sector's delivery of education (Verger et al., 2016). Beyond elite universities profitable institutional engagement within domestic and global economies, they also provide an attractive means for dominant nations to extending their power and domination of economic fields beyond their national economies.

Bourdieu suggests, 'the "global market" is a political creation' (2005: 225); so just as inequitable distributions of capitals have determined domestic economies, with increasing globalisation the relationship and positioning of nation states are determined by the pre-existing inequitable distribution of capitals. As economies and populations change the potential for states who are already disadvantaged to adapt is limited by the interests of already dominant nations. The model for the global market therefore is never a free-market economy driven by laws of supply and demand but rather an economy shaped by the dominant interests of already dominant nations preserving and protecting their status. Whilst a free market assumes everyone benefits from trade this is curtailed by the interests of dominant nations. A process that is exacerbated by the production of knowledge within elite universities that both presumes its own ascendancy and also has the means to promote and confirm its greater symbolic value on the global stage. The forms of knowledge produced by western, elite universities are legitimised by a means of production in which a small block of super-elite universities maintain the ultimate regulatory control. The brands of these universities act as seals of approval to validate the status of knowledge produced globally.

Bourdieu (2005) notes this global reach mirrors previous domination of national markets and this perhaps underlines the failed promise of globalisation not just for those outside of America or Europe but also those already living in those countries with less access to capitals. The promise of a more fluid or liquid global economy and of individuals reflexively managing newly found cosmopolitan identities (Beck, 1992; Beck et al., 2003; Bauman, 2000a) feels at odds with the realities of austerity politics driven by neoliberal policy-making top benefit a handful of already well-placed individuals, institutions and commercial concerns. Instead a process of domination of subordinate national economies by wealthier, more powerful states occurs. This mirrors the momentum of powerful institutions and ideology within already powerful nation states and the struggle for position individually within those institutions.

The role of elite university brands associated with highly valued cultural capital in the global 'market' becomes a means of legitimating domestic political authority globally. The often narrow geographical locations (e.g. Cambridge, Massachusetts or Oxford), in which university brands are shaped seemingly adding scarcity value to the brand. These processes become apparent as universities market educational packages tethered to pre-existing national understandings of institutional value (Friedman, 2017) in which local geographies represent added value in the competition to cater for global student markets (McCarthy and Kenway, 2014). Eastwood (2012), discussing his experience as Vice Chancellor of a well-placed Russell Group university, suggests this investment in place is a more general feature of universities in which specific bilateral relationships between geography and the type of provision emerge. Such relationships are inevitably restricted to the sub-field of elite and high-ranking institutions. The cachet of Oxford and the University of Oxford is a specific bilateral relationship; one that, despite its proximity, is not shared with Oxford Brookes University. As universities expand their global reach with online MOOCs,[5] international collaborations and overseas campuses, it is still the local spaces of universities that embody their character, identity and brand. In this respect the 'Harvard experience is Harvard in Cambridge Massachusetts. However generous it is with its online content, that is not the Harvard experience, but a tantalising fragment of it, offered out of context. Not valueless of course, but different' (Eastwood, 2012: 35).

Bourdieu notes that the 'limits of the field' is itself *'always at stake in the field itself'* (1992: 100). For ambitious, global elite universities seeking to expand their influence, the limits of the field might be determined locally, nationally and globally because of the relational and competitive nature of institutions and their agents to dominate across and through different fields. At a local level the competition between established, traditional players (wealthy elites perhaps whose parents attended the same institutions) and newer allegiances (students from poorer or more diverse ethnic backgrounds promoting newer discourses such as 'widening participation'), relates to the acquisition and redistribution of capitals within the institution. It also determines how institutions will deploy their pre-existing, highly privileged national cultural capital to acquire greater influence across global economic fields. Despite the difficulty in pinning down its material attributes the elite university brand is one of the stakes students compete to acquire; both in the legitimation it gives to their university credentials and the access it opens to productive social networks.

The Cosmopolitan Brand: Local and Global Elite Capital

A recurrent theme to emerge from students' accounts of elite universities was their perception of their institution's global reach related to personal ambitions for careers played out on a global stage. This mirrored the privileged dispositions of ascendant elites or 'haves' identified by Bauman (2000a, 2000b), who are free to move across borders in pursuit of work, pleasure or economic gain as compared to 'have nots', who move because they are forced to. Both domestic and international students suggested a significant factor in the value they derived from studying at an elite university was the instant global recognition of their degree and the credentialised cultural capital attached to its possessor. Reflecting on her previous experience studying in America, international student Gargi noted the significance of the brand to access global opportunities because of the types of cultural capital she had accumulated,

> The name will get me far. It has already established me to have access to great opportunities in Europe and internationally around the world. I can take that with me everywhere I go. Having that marks you out from everyone, it gives you so much standing and credentials that are worth a lot in many different

ways. It says certain things about you as a person – and not just about your education, your class and your access to people.

Home students also identified the value of institutional brands, Ralf noting the potential impact US1 might have for him,

> I know that I can use the name and take it anywhere in the world and use it to my advantage, it will be recognised and there will be others who are in similar positions. I was able to do an internship at a major company in my first year and all the other interns had been to an elite university – as had most of the people working there – the idea that the name is global makes an impact.

Students identified the exclusivity of institutional brands and their global currency but also highlighted more nebulous traits emblematic of institutions' global brand recognisability that were often rooted in its local, physical spaces. Georgina (British, UK2) described a dining hall that was 'Harry Potterworld in the flesh'; and many students echoed the sentiments of Edward (American, US2) who spoke of, 'coach loads of tourists from China and elsewhere going to the university shop to buy branded hoodies and other paraphernalia'. Describing his experience as an undergraduate at another Ivy League institution Tony noted 'they look similar. All the green spaces and the red buildings. They look similar and they feel the same'.

A picture emerged of global brands defined by their name, reputation, imagery and the weight of influence afforded their exclusive membership. Almost all respondents (even those who questioned their privilege and advantage) suggested they would use the brand to further their own careers and prospects, indicating the degree of complicity between students and the university social space (Bourdieu and Wacquant, 1992). Tony identified how he would 'capitalise on the brand name',

> You don't have to explain it, you don't have to explain what it means. It's just known, it's a brand. I guess it's like saying Chanel or something. Everyone knows what Chanel is, who doesn't know?

For other students learning to be a part of the brand did not come naturally. Zena (American, US1) had not previously attended an elite university and described feeling 'ill at ease' studying at US1; suggesting this was partly a consequence of expectations of how students position themselves and exhibit the dispositions of the university's global identity,

> How [US1] is understood is universal, how elite is understood is also universal. The brand is seen as the most valuable. It's transferable and known all over the world. It's based on having a certain style, a certain way of doing things; speaking, thinking and even writing and if you don't conform to that you will find it hard to fit in. It's about learning the culture here and how it

works. The language is all part of that, how you speak with the professors and how you interact with the other students.

Whilst Zena identified local practices that shaped the brand in the image of the institutional social space, Femi placed greater significance on the work the brand was doing to shape student identities. Within the relational social spaces of universities, the effectiveness of global, elite brands is predicated around transferring and maintaining regimes of power that privilege and advance the interests of those from the university. Within these dynamics are variations in how capitals are transferred and accumulated driven by individual *habitus* and access to capitals. Femi described patterns of social behaviours, individual characteristics and competition for resources at UK2 that mirrors Bourdieusian accounts of university fields (Bourdieu and Wacquant, 1992); but additionally identified the potency of the brand itself and how it almost operates as an active agent,

> It is the reputation that exists that is over and above the actual quality of the education. The advantage of being here has to do with the name. As a [UK2] student, it opens up doors and gives you access to networks, but it's the name that opens up the doors. But by the same token the name and brand can also be a problem, because you have to conform to the brand and know what is expected of you. You have to be good in a certain kind of way, you have to have a certain kind of brilliance.

Being a student of an elite university was often compared to membership of an exclusive club that provided access to, and compatibility with, the exclusivity of its brand. Simon (British, US2) described discomfort between less privileged backgrounds and elite university experiences that echoed earlier respondents but he also specifically linked this to the university brand,

> The brand gives you and provides you with entrance into exclusive spaces, which leads to other exclusive spaces. This space has a hierarchy based on how intelligent and interesting you are. The name also gives you super confidence that you can't get from anywhere else. It's like saying, well if [US2] thinks I'm good enough then I must be really good and I can use that and exploit it to get what I want.

For Simon the brand of US2 was linked directly to the cultural capital that was being fostered and competed for locally within the university. It was cultural capital that he understood to privilege the legitimacy to his future claim to being an elite global citizen.

Throughout our discussions with students at elite universities there was a noticeable self-reflexivity on the part of students. For some this materialised specifically in their identification of problems associated with elite universities around inequality, unfairness and a sense of discomfort with their positioning. All the students we interviewed identified that attending these universities bestowed advantages upon them, and for many students their engagement within a globally, recognised elite brand was a valuable asset in their futures. According to Juan (American, US2),

> US2 is marketed as an elite brand and that's what it is. Once you say the name, there are certain things attached to it. It gives you a magical bubble of opportunities that you would not otherwise have access to.

Conclusions

Students identified a range of relationships between their past experiences (particularly educational), current engagement as graduate students at elite universities and expectations for the future. These relationships were foregrounded on pre-existing characteristics including knowledge of how the university brand worked, and the personal advantages bestowed by the brand. Unusually, what also emerged, was evidence of the cosmopolitan nature of global elite university brands; the struggle for capitals and position happened at a local level, in institutions steeped in recognisably local geographies and histories. However, acquisition of cultural capital and the legitimisation of student's capitals were intrinsic to the brand's global reach. By generating new cohorts of students endowed with the local currency of its brand, the potential for a brand's global legitimacy was effectively reproduced and extended.

Elite universities generate a legitimacy around the types of cultural capital they produce that is 'taken for granted' and reflects the established '*doxa*' (Bourdieu, 1977: 166). This natural social ordering underpins understandings of which roles are suited to which people, shaped by an unspoken perception of the deployment of individual's characteristics and traits within different fields (Bourdieu and Wacquant, 1992). For elite universities this legitimacy, so apparent in their global brands, is also imbued in the experiences of its graduate students who are complicit in local, institutional competitions for position and status; processes in which they are continually demonstrating their congruity with established orders. The global brand's legitimacy, its currency, is embedded in the local institutional competition for its capitals. This is a mutually benefitting process. Elite universities deploy their 'brands' and their 'people'; by doing so, asserting the ascendancy of their cultural capital to position their institutions at the forefront of American-Anglo strategies to maintain and extend economic power globally. For graduate students the brand's legitimacy bestows personal legitimacy and a 'taken for granted' status within competition for the acquisition of capitals. As elite universities extend their pre-existing ascendancy within their national social, political and economic hierarchies on a global stage; their graduate students are also increasingly global actors.

Graduate students invariably described both an awareness of their institutions' global brands; and also, the pressurised, competitive local processes shaping their time at university. Their general complicity in these processes in no small part reflected their awareness of the personal rewards that accrued from the brand. For all the graduate students the global brand of the elite university was a sign of their legitimate credentialised capital, confirmed by their presence within the field of a global elite university. For those best positioned, because of prior dispositions or pre-existing access to capitals, the scale of reward was envisaged to be higher and more accessible. Students from more privileged backgrounds were Bourdieu's (1986) 'fish in water'; they were at home in university spaces. They had a *feel* for the brand and its opportunities.

The ease with which some students navigated elite universities whilst those from less privileged backgrounds often struggled highlights the enduring importance of local, domestic competition to retain and acquire capitals. Graduate students were engaged in a multitude of relational positionings that included building social networks and acquiring credentials. Perhaps most significantly, they appeared positioned in terms of their competition for legitimacy; the competition for cultural capital that confirmed their right to the brand and the status it conferred. That branded legitimacy would have the biggest impact on their future acquisition of cultural, social and economic capitals through their progression into high-status employment.

This local competition highlights the cosmopolitan nature of elite university brands to privilege specific students, particularly those already privileged. Whilst the brand is understood in terms of globally recognised logos, rankings and influence; it is shaped by a local university *ethos* encompassing how its members behave and think, teach and learn. A picture emerged from the accounts graduate students gave of their pathways to elite universities, experiences whilst there and hopes for the future; in which particular types of student are imbued with cultural capital that has global legitimacy. This *elite corps* acquires access to a global brand, enabling them to secure positions of privilege and advantage once they have left the university. Amongst themselves an ongoing local struggle is apparent in which the personal stakes of competing for a bigger slice of the brand are tempered by pre-existing access to capitals in particular the access to legitimacy imbued in more privileged backgrounds. Historically the brands of elite universities might have been predominantly deployed to ensure power and influence was retained within domestic settings; increasingly cosmopolitan brands ensure a similar group of people extend and maintain their power globally.

Notes

1 All Conditions Gear.
2 Nike Sport Lab Research.
3 Oxford Brooks University, formerly Oxford Polytechnic, was granted university status in 1992. Although geographically close to Oxford University it has a more modest status and reputation.
4 The Ivy League are eight prestigious private US universities. All but one pre-date the American Revolution and they are characterised by exceptionally large endowment funds. Oxbridge is the colloquial term for the Universities of Cambridge and Oxford, the two oldest, most prestigious and wealthiest UK universities. The Russell Group consists of 24 research intensive UK universities consistently placed highly in league tables.
5 Massive Open Online Courses.

8
WHITE CAPITAL AND THE MAINTENANCE OF WHITE SUPREMACY

There is long-standing and widespread evidence to suggest that students of colour experience racism and prejudice, a white curriculum, poor academic outcomes and have difficulty adjusting to the white space of elite universities (Bhopal, 2018; Charles et al., 2004; EHRC, 2019; Pilkington, 2011; 2012; Torres and Charles 2004; Torres, 2009; UUK/NUS, 2019; Willie, 2003). This is a consequence of a constellation of factors that disadvantage students of colour. As shown in Chapter 6, although students spoke of their distinct, individual experiences and perceptions of racism in elite universities, they also highlighted a recognisable backdrop of racist practices that affected their experiences. We argue that whiteness as a defining characteristic of elite universities is embodied within forms of capital that determine student outcomes. Whiteness as a form of power lies at the heart of elite universities core structural procedures and values. Simultaneously, whiteness is embodied as valuable within the individual characteristics of all social actors associated with elite universities, including graduate students.

This chapter takes as its starting point the centrality of racism in the experiences of graduate students at elite universities. We understand racism to be a 'normal, not aberrant' feature of everyday life, and consequently, one that 'looks ordinary and natural to persons in the culture' (Delgado and Stefancic, 2000: 12). The normalcy of racism within society, and within the spaces of elite universities, was readily apparent in the accounts of our participants. We draw upon critical race theory (CRT) understandings of whiteness as means of analysing how racism in elite universities affects graduate students. As shown in earlier chapters the experiences of different students are deeply personal and individual. The field of the elite university is a dynamic and changing space of social relations in which individual students' experiences are often affected by multiple divergent and changing inequalities. This reflects the nature of race itself as socially constructed categories that are fluid rather than unchanging classifications specific to temporal–spatial

DOI: 10.4324/9781003029922-8

circumstances (Gillborn, 2008). CRT provides a useful lens because it emphasises the need to contextualise individual experiential accounts (Delgado and Stefancic, 2000; Tate, 1997).

Despite its nomenclature CRT is primarily a set of shared approaches to understanding race and racism in contemporary society rather than a single theoretical position; though it often deploys specific theoretical tools such as 'intersectionality' and 'interest convergence'. It emerged out of, and in response to, the progressive scholarship of critical legal studies (CLS) in the US associated with a left-liberal critique of American society and support for the civil rights movement. CRT scholars identified that within CLS there was an absence of understanding of race and racism. Rather than identifying the distinct inequalities defined by race and racism, CLS tended to amalgamate racism within generic accounts of inequality specifically framed by class and gender. Bearing in mind the foundations of modern America in contexts of colonialism and slavery this absence spoke to failures within progressive politics. CRT provides a critique of progressive liberal politics in which the normalcy of racism is readily overlooked. Ladson-Billings and Tate (1995) identified that race, unlike class and gender, was not theorised within educational scholarship and that the theoretical approaches to understanding class and gender inequalities did not address issues of racial inequality within education. Noting the centrality of racism to CRT and its multi-disciplinary approach Tate (1997) identifies three other key features of CRT for educational research. First, it identifies that legal remedies addressing inequality are often stymied before being effectively implemented. In the US this is exemplified by the *Brown v. Board of education* (1954) ruling to end segregated public schooling. Despite *Brown v. Board of education*, subsequent segregated schooling persisted but was engineered by other means including racial neighbourhood zoning (Rosiek, 2019; Trounstine, 2020). In the UK Gillborn demonstrates comparable retrenchment of pre-existing racism within educational policy that has 'pandered to White racist sentiment and left the principal race inequalities untouched' (Gillborn, 2008: 89). Second, Tate suggests that CRT recognises the 'dominant legal claims of neutrality, objectivity, color blindness, and meritocracy as camouflages for the self-interest of powerful entities of society' (Tate, 1997: 235). The dominant narratives of much educational discourse suggest students' success is determined by personal attributes rather than family background; this is evidentially untrue as persistently demonstrated in almost all credible educational research (Bhopal, 2018; Reay, 2017). However, the language of these narratives invariably draws upon terminology understood to be inclusive rather than exclusive, equitable rather than inequitable; that despite its tone persistently underpins the reproduction of inequalities. Finally, Tate (1997) argues that CRT can address the ahistoricism at the heart of much education policy, in particular by recognising and valuing the experiential accounts of people who are often excluded from the discourse.

Whiteness and White Capital

The significance of whiteness as a category and form of power has been widely identified (Dyer, 1988; 1997; Frankenberg, 1993; Hurtado, 1996; Hooks, 1997; Ignatiev, 1995; Kidder, 1997; McIntosh, 1992; Roediger, 1991; 2002) including research in educational settings in the US (Apple, 1998; Giroux, 1997; Kincheloe and Steinberg, 1998; Sleeter, 1996) and the UK (Chakrabarty et al., 2016; Gillborn, 2005; Preston, 2007; Warmington, 2014). Much of this work identifies how the ethnicity of white groups works as a form of privilege. McIntosh (1992) in her work explores how whiteness and white privilege are based on the possession of a set privileges which work like an invisible rucksack that white people carry on their backs. Additionally, Leonardo argues that 'a critical look at white privilege, or the analysis of white racial hegemony, must be complemented by an equally rigorous examination of white supremacy, or the analysis of white racial domination' (2009: 75). The relationships between *white privilege*, *white supremacy* and *white racial domination* centre around the processes by which racism is legitimised and understood to be a normal feature of social organisation.

Preston argues that white ethnicity is 'a political category that is historically and socially reproduced over time' (2007: 2). Despite identifying the ambiguities associated with categories such as *white*, *White* and *Whiteness*, Preston argues, 'it is not fully accurate to describe whiteness as a contested term. Rather it is a combative term across which a number of disputes are gathered regarding the nature of race in general' (2007: 2). Consequently within political discourse the specific identification of who is and who is not white changes over time; but this is a political discourse that always maintains the ascendancy of whiteness. In part this explains the Irish American experience in which the first Irish migrants to the US held roughly the same status as the Black population but transitioned to becoming an ascendant white group (Ignatiev, 1995). The Irish experience was socially constructed within the broader pattern of migration from rural European to the US urban environments in which immigrants were categorised within a,

> moral hierarchy of national and cultural differences in which the Western Europeans – with the exception of the Irish – stood at the top, diligent, hard-working, and for the most part, skilled laborers, and in which Slavs, Bohemians, Jews and Southern Europeans stood lower, accused of dirtiness, secretiveness or laziness.
>
> *(Sennet and Cobb, 1972: 14)*

Just as the example of Irish migrants transcending their initial low status demonstrates whiteness reproducing itself in new socio-economic circumstances that maintain white ascendancy, the opposite may also hold true. Hartigan (1997) discusses how the term 'white trash' is used to categorise some white groups. In previously respectable white middle-class suburbs affected by downward mobility, 'white trash' are held accountable for 'disrupting implicit understandings of what it means to be white. Here, white trash designates ruptures of conventions that maintain whiteness as an unmarked, normative identity' (Hartigan, 1997: 46). 'White trash' as a stigmatising insult, 'constitutes more than a derogatory exchange of name calling; it materializes a complicated policing of the inchoate boundaries that comprise class and racial identities' (Hartigan, 1997: 47). In the UK, the same delineation of whiteness that distinguishes the acceptability of respectable white identities from other, racialised identities can be seen in the use of terminology such as 'chavs'.[1]

Whilst the emergence of 'white trash' or 'chavs' signals white identities are neither homogenous nor fixed, it does not suggest that whiteness itself is devalued. Rather it provides further evidence that whiteness is a social construct in which race should be 'understood as a differential system of advantage that benefits all whites regardless of their class or gender status' (Leonardo, 2009: 69). Gillborn (2008) argues that although structural processes perpetuate whiteness as a means to oppress and marginalise ethnic minorities; within those processes individual white groups and individual white people are complicit in maintaining a system, which benefits their own positions. Gillborn states, 'Whiteness matters. CRT does not assume that all White people are the same . . . but CRT does argue that all White people are implicated in White supremacy' (Gillborn, 2008: 34). In the context of elite universities, populated by heterogeneous groups that can be delineated along multiple characteristics including race, class, gender and academic and non-academic status; whiteness remains a defining characteristic of both individuals and institutional structures.

Whiteness as Property

Students of colour experience pressure in predominantly white university environments where a lack of cultural capital, specifically the forms of cultural capital disproportionately available to white students, disadvantages them (Carter, 2003; 2005; Torres, 2009). Types of capital act as forms of power within their specific fields (Horvat, 2003; Bourdieu, 1986; 1996) and the most valuable and effective forms of capital are those that integrate most closely with the field itself. White cultural capital is more aligned to the field of elite universities than the capital of students of colour, not least because it reflects the majoritarian interests of middle-class white academics, students and their parents.

In her account of 'white privilege' McIntosh (1992) describes how white people possess a set of privileges that they can carry around with them in their daily lives. One reason the possession of white privilege is so effective is its invisibility; the benefits it delivers seem unremarkable and consequently not worthy of being challenged. As a form of white supremacy it is an effective means of denying the existence of racism and its impact on the lives of people of colour (Bonilla-Silva, 2002; 2006; Omni and Winant, 1994). Universities have been identified as 'both a site of whiteness normalization and disruption' (Cabrera, 2014: 31). So despite being a field in which structural racism in particular, is increasingly identified and challenged; universities are still spaces where students often self-segregate and perform overtly racist behaviours such as 'blacking up parties'. Cabrera suggests that university campuses are spaces in which, 'manifestations of white privilege allow the participants to enact racist stereotypes in relatively safe environments separate from their minority peers' (2014: 33). Although some white students display 'cultural envy' of their Black peers, McKinney (2004) argues that white students take their whiteness, and white supremacy, for granted and maintain their distance from minority students. Torres (2009) identifies a range of behaviours and characteristics that distinguish white students from students of colour. This includes white students making critical comments about black bodies and black sexuality; different dress codes; segregated social lives and account of different tastes and styles. Torres (2009) also notes that this is framed in the context of Black students often coming from less affluent backgrounds than their white peers and described the 'culture shock' of students hailing from predominantly Black or mixed neighbourhoods encountering the white spaces of universities.

The evident disparity in types of cultural capital often finds its materialisation in practices that devalue students of colour. In this sense the *taken for granted* value attached to whiteness is potentially challenged by the presence of students of colour. In particular, if students are admitted to elite universities that portray meritocratic neutrality as part of their narrative of equity when selecting the *best* students. Within the field of elite universities challenges to the *status quo*, such as evidence students are being admitted who do not possess the requisite characteristic of whiteness, results in adaptations to reassert the dominant interests of white communities. This includes the deployment and competition for cultural capital to assert the status and value of whiteness as a racialised property. One example of such white supremacy has been evident in claims that students of colour gain admission as a result of favourable admissions processes rather than on the basis of merit (Feagin, Vera and Imani, 2014; 1996). Cabrera (2014) found that white males in the US college campus felt they were under attack from affirmative action initiatives which they identified as evidence that minority communities were racist towards white people. The white men in Cabrera's study did not acknowledge their own racial privilege or consider their investment in racially segregated environments as problematic. Their perception of being the victims of *reverse racism*, 'tended to be framed as rational interpretations of objective realities' (2014: 50). However, this objective reality was constructed within the limits of a narrow white world view in which, 'their white privilege allowed them to racially insulate, concurrently denying the power of racism in contemporary society' (2014: 51).

Statistical evidence to support claims of racial bias is problematic to generate in part because they need to allow for a range of potentially competing indicators (Morris, 2018). So, for example, it is not just the number of offers made by universities that needs to be considered, but also the types of offer, acceptances of offer, subject area and institutional type. In the UK, policy that has prioritised widening participation is often hailed as a success because of the evidence of increasing numbers of non-traditional students. However, on closer examination of the data and of students experiences it becomes apparent that non-traditional students are far more likely to attend less prestigious universities, often 'assuming a relative parity between different institutions and the value of their degrees. Students of colour, without the initial access to capitals generally enter into a lesser game with lower stakes than those with an excess of capitals' (Bhopal et al., 2020: 1333). This is further exacerbated by the current funding arrangements for UK students who pay the same fee (often by means of a student loan), regardless of institutional type. Consequently students attending the most prestigious, elite universities (a population heavily skewed towards the white, middle class) pay the same as students attending less prestigious, local universities. The final degree qualification of the elite university holds greater credential value than those of less prestigious universities. It is likely to result in greater returns in the employment market, for example. In essence however, students at more or less prestigious universities are required to make the same economic investment in the cost of their differently valued degrees. In this model, 'the transfer of economic capital mirrors transfers of knowledge and cultural capital, and the fostering of social networks to benefit already privileged students. Put simply, students from poorer, non-traditional working-class BME backgrounds pay more and get less back' (Bhopal et al., 2020: 1333). In the US, Harvard University faced legal challenges that its admissions processes favoured Black and Hispanic admissions whilst restricting access for Asian students (Hartocollis, 2020). In 2020 the United States District Court for the District of Massachusetts concluded the university did not discriminate in its admissions process, the case has since been referred to the Supreme Court.

Whiteness and Belonging

Many students of colour from less affluent backgrounds expressed feelings of doubt about their right to belong within elite university spaces. They often doubted whether their legitimacy to be at elite universities was recognised by middle-class peers and their professors. The doubts felt by students of colour about their presence within elite universities reflected personal narratives of discomfort. One apparent irony was that their discontent remained constant despite the overwhelming claim of elite universities that they were meritocratic institutions. In principle, by gaining a place as a graduate student at an elite university, students should experience affirmation of their ability and right to belong. However students of colour in our research tended not to describe that outcome but instead continued to express doubts about their belonging.

A number of students of colour described their white peers openly suggesting that their ethnicity gave them a favourable advantage by being part of '*the quota*', benefitting from '*special measures*' or a '*tick box exercise*'. This was a means by which the collective meritocratic narrative of elite universities could be maintained whilst simultaneously undermining the credentials of individual students who did not possess forms of white capital. Some students also suggested they were 'allowed' to be at an elite university because it benefitted the university by presenting a façade of institutional inclusivity to the outside world; rather than a genuine engagement with widening participation policies.

Nema, a Black working-class student, described how her peers made jokes about her benefitting from affirmative action policies at US1 and then explained this produced lingering doubts about whether or not she deserved to be at US1,

> Sometimes I do wonder whether I am filling a quota. Whether I got here because of some sort of affirmative action measure or other such special measure. And I feel I am sometimes made to feel that way by my peers and sometimes my professors. Even though I did go to an Ivy League university as an undergraduate there is still that sense that *how come you came here?* When I'm asked that question. And even professors ask it, "*how come you came here?*" It's not a simple question, its always about who I am and what's my story. I have been told so many thousands of students apply for the programme here and only a small handful, literally a small handful, get in. So we must be here for some other reason.

Zena whose family was from Afghanistan and from a working-class background felt that her presence in US1 was also, always questioned by others. Consequently she also questioned herself about why she was a student at US2,

> I am made to feel that this isn't my space and when that happens I begin to question it myself. One of my classmates has actually said to me that the reason the faculty has more students of colour is because they have to fill their quota and they have to adhere to affirmative action laws because otherwise US1 will look bad. So when a student openly says this to you; you are made to question why are you here? You may be thinking I am here because I can think critically and fall into that category of students who are the chosen ones who have got a place at US1. But then you question that and think well maybe I am here because I am filling a quota and maybe I am here because US1 wants the outside world, the global world to think they are inclusive. Rather than wanting students from diverse backgrounds because this is important.

Ria who was mixed heritage (Indian/white) and working class also described how perceptions that she was favourably treated by the admissions process because of her ethnicity had an ongoing impact on how she felt about her status at UK1. Much like Nema, she identified that other students' perceptions of her sowed doubts about the legitimacy of her place at an elite university,

> UK1 is considered one of two *best* universities in the world, so someone like me wonders how you got here. I have to keep thinking that I'm here because I am bright and I got here because of my grades. But when I have spoken to students who have been to prep school, to private school they question

me. They wonder why I am here? Some have the cheek to do it openly but others do it in subtle ways. When they ask which school did you go to and you tell them just an ordinary *comp*[2] they just look at you and assume you are here because you have ticked a box. So I do wonder whether the university wants to have the odd working class student, the odd Black student and the odd BME student so they can say, 'look at us, we are diverse'. So it makes them look good, makes them look like they are contributing to making UK1 accessible to all students, but in reality they are doing it for themselves. They don't really care about us because we are not like them.

Ria and Zena both identified forms of cultural capital associated with whiteness that benefitted white students within elite universities. Although narratives of affirmative action policies were inaccurate and did not reflect evidence that students of colour were less likely to be successfully admitted to elite universities; they still retained a significant currency amongst white students. This was a narrative that devalued the capitals of students of colour and reasserted the greater value of capitals held by white students. The willingness of some white students to openly make such claims, sometimes couched as jokes, demonstrates white capital's effectiveness as a dominant form of power within the elite university. By doing so they were undermining the sense of belonging of students of colour by casting doubt on the legitimacy of their credentials, in particular academic credentials. Whiteness is a valuable property within the elite university because it protects the overriding interests of the dominant population. It is a property that both cements white students belief in their rightful entitlement to inhabit the university and also protects and fosters the value that can be drawn from an elite university by undermining students who are not white.

In Ria's account she makes the additional comment that whilst she recognises the lack of legitimisation she experiences because white students make the claim she benefits from an inequitable process; at the same time, the university actively proclaims its commitment to diversity is emblematic of their egalitarian ethos. In effect, the narrative of diversity is used by white students to undermine the capital possessed by students of colour; and contemporaneously the white university bolsters its capitals by highlighting its diversity. Institutional social dynamics actively counter the potential implementation of equity measures.

Femi went further than Ria, explicitly suggesting the only reason UK2 admitted Black working-class students like herself, was to benefit by appearing inclusive to the outside world.

I have to keep telling myself that I am here because I *deserve* to be here, because I got the grades, because I performed well in the interview and because I am clever enough to be here. But then I see all these people in power. The VC and the PVC's going on about how they think it's important to have a more diverse student body etc. But I can't help but think they are only doing this to look good in the public eye. They want the world to look at UK2 and think it's inclusive and diverse, but in reality they are only doing them for their own ends and not because they really want Black students who aren't posh to come here. They want to just keep it white and posh and everything else is just a façade.

In his analysis of *Brown v. Board of education*, Bell (1980) famously and controversially suggested the legal argument for the desegregation of public schools only happened because it was in the interests of white people to do so. He noted that the turning point in legislating against segregated schools coincided with US foreign policy interests competition for influence with the Soviet Union in third-world countries that were hampered by the US reputation for racial violence; with the return of Black servicemen after the Second World War disillusioned by the persistence racism at home and unlikely to fight again for the US; and, finally that the continued segregation of the South was hindering its industrialisation and commercial development. Desegregation of public schools was therefore more beneficial for white people both nationally and globally than maintaining resources to benefit white-only schools. The implementation of desegregated schooling was a contested and long-drawn-out process and one that in practice has not delivered desegregated schools (Feagin and Barnett, 2004; Rosiek, 2019; Trounstine, 2020). Bell describes the Brown v. Board decision as an example of 'interest convergence'. Accounts such as Femi's of elite universities embracing diversity can be understood as a similar example of interest convergence. Throughout our research elite universities were consistently identified as exclusive institutions serving white middle-class interests. At the same time there was also a flourishing of radical political interventions challenging universities for their poor record addressing structural and institutional racism. It became increasingly paramount that universities distanced themselves from evidence of their long-standing inequitable admissions processes and inability to address instances of racism within university life.

Affluence, Whiteness and Meritocracy

For more affluent students of colour the suggestion that admissions processes made allowances because of their ethnicity was often challenged. Whereas less affluent students described doubts engendered by such narratives, middle-class students of colour in our study did not share the same feelings. They often made similar claims to those of affluent white students about their right to study at an elite university. Some students also made specific claims about seeing themselves as sharing closer characteristics and interests with their white middle-class peers rather than less affluent students.

Tom a Black student studying at US1 identified coming from a 'comfortable, well-off' family. He previously completed his undergraduate studies at another elite university and both his parents were successful professionals. Discussing affirmative action policies and admissions processes Tom explained that,

> I know I am here because I have earned my place to be here. I have made it here because I worked hard. It's like entering a competition, when you win you don't think you won because someone felt sorry for you or because they wanted you to win because you are from some background. It doesn't work like that.

Tom went on to discuss the impact of affirmative action policy as a generally positive feature of US2 and elite universities. However, he was very clear they were not significant factors in his own academic trajectory.

> I know about those quotas and affirmative action, but that isn't for people like me, it's for people who maybe haven't had the opportunities that others have. They might be say, from poor backgrounds with poor schools and so US2 compensates for people like that. But for me, it wasn't about that I didn't come from that sort of background.

Tom explicitly understood that his place at US1 was not related to his race or ethnicity, and additionally, that this was well-understood by other students and academics. The parallels he drew with other students highlighted similarities with other white and Black middle-class students. In many respects Tom appeared to separate his ethnic identity from his class identity, aligning his interests with wealthy, white middle-class students rather than Black students more generally. Like many of the more affluent students, Tom was confident to describe his belief in his academic ability. He also explicitly suggested his personal narrative reflected aspects associated with whiteness,

> My being here is about my achievements, it's part of my journey and that journey is the same as my white peers. I am in the same category as them, we all had a similar upbringing and so we are all on the same trajectory. It's not about your racial background, it's more about who can achieve and get to the top. We are in the same position because we have had the same sort of opportunities. Those students who are here because of quotas are different, they have not had the same opportunities.

Tom readily equated quotas or affirmative action policies with poverty and that these were underpinned by the association with race. Although his perception of US1 still stressed its meritocratic underpinnings this did not extend to assuming that a privileged background contributed to easing, either his own or others, access to an elite university. Consequently he explained that poorer students were as academically capable as other students but effectively disadvantaged by the educational system. In essence he believed in the legitimacy of his own more privilege background rather than perhaps concluding affirmative action was a means of challenging such inherent privilege,

I think those students who have got here because of some sort of special measure are bright enough to be here, but they needed that help to get here. Once they are here, they have to show they are as good as us, because they have to keep up with us.

When Tom referred to 'us' he was identifying students like himself from wealthy backgrounds with parents working in well-paid professions who anticipated attending an Ivy League university because it was the norm. His description of this category included implicit assumptions that whiteness was also a likely characteristic and that an alternative category of students benefitting from affirmative action was characterised by poverty and being Black.

A number of differences delineated Tom's experience from less affluent Black students including his feelings of belonging and being at home within the US1 environment. Unlike less affluent students, he did not provide accounts of feeling excluded from the white norms of the university.

Another student with a comparable background was Edward. He was at US2 and previously studied at another Ivy League university and both his parents were in professional occupations. When asked directly which students he identified with, Edward responded,

I do identify with my African American students because we are Black, but then I feel more at home with my white students who have had similar experiences to me. Some of my students who were at the same college as me are here and they are white. They have the same sort of experiences I have, the same interests and so we bond. We play the same sports and we do the same sort of things. I don't think that they are white and I am Black, they are just my friends.

Edward's colour-blind perspective suggested that the things that bind him with his peers are his interests and similarities. Although race was a constituent part of those characteristics, it appeared to be filtered out by more significant characteristics such as shared interests. These shared characteristics appeared to be defined within white forms of capital, including prior access to wealth; as opposed to Black forms of capital associated with poverty. Edward and Tom (and other Black middle-class students), use wealth and their middle-class tastes to distinguish themselves from Black working-class students. They differentiate themselves from specific forms of Black capital and by doing so exclude other Black students from their more privileged spaces. In doing so, they identify more with their white middle-class peers. Andre who was mixed heritage (Black/white) at US2 and from a middle-class background said this explicitly,

It's being able to share those experiences that some students have and others do not, like the things that we have all done. Some of the students who may not have been to those clubs or done those things won't get it. So you end up being friends with people who are like you, who have had the same backgrounds. My dad studied here and I know other students whose parents studied here. So you naturally navigate to them, they get it. I don't choose my friends because of their racial background. I choose them because we have things in common. They just happen to be white.

Andre's colour-blind perspective was exclusive in that his friends who were white or Black were all, like himself, from middle-class wealthy backgrounds.

In the UK a different picture emerged in which race was identified as a more significant factor than class. Middle-class students of colour were more likely to describe identifying with other students based on their race, rather than their class. At the time the research was being conducted elite universities were engaged in ongoing discourses around their exclusivity and inclusiveness. This included both student-led activism often focused on highlighting historic connections between universities and the slave trade and institutional responses as such as decolonising the curriculum. The issue of quotas or affirmative action to recruit by race or ethnicity was not identified to the same degree; however, universities were discussed as sites in which complex contestations around race and racism were an everyday feature.

Andrew who was mixed heritage (Black/white) and from a middle-class background identified that racism was a significant issue at UK2, not least because it was 'making front page news on a pretty regular basis' explained that,

> It is evident that UK2 is racist, there are lots of examples of how students of colour are treated and how staff are treated and some of these have been high profile. Here we know that regardless of where we have come from we are not accepted here, so we try and do what we can to ensure that we support each other. We have a BAME[3] students' network and BAME student campaign and we all come together in these networks. We don't look at the things that make us different we try and unite together.

Andrew's contention that racism was an overt feature of university life was widely shared by other students. He cited the evidence of his own and other comparable universities poor record of recruiting students of colour, direct instances of racist behaviour towards students of colour and the disproportionately small number of senior academics of colour. He also made the point that these issues were well-documented,

> It's on the news. And social media all the time. [UK2] has a terrible reputation at the moment. My gut instinct says the university is very nervous because they cannot offload the blame. In the past it would be the schools fault, or the government or the parents. But no one buys that any more.

Andrew went on to suggest that the recruitment process for funded graduate roles at UK2 was deliberately ambiguous in order to privilege white students,

We just never know what the actual metric is. The specific criteria to be offered a place. No one knows because it all happens in a conversation behind closed doors. There is no shortage of students with top grades. No shortage of very bright, smart, ambitious people at all. When the decisions happen obviously no one says, "take the white guy". But the whole process is premised on identifying [UK2] people. People like us.

Another student who also identified the ambiguous relationship between merito-cratic criteria such as A Level[4] grades and the realities of being offered a place was Daphne. She identified as mixed heritage (white/Indian) and middle class at UK1. She described how the recruitment of undergraduates also allowed universities to pick and choose students based on institutional preferences,

The way you get a place here as an undergraduate is to some extent flawed. Yes you have to get the grades, but there is also the interview and the entrance test. If you don't make those, then you don't get in. The students in my cohort have all been to a top university and are now studying here as a post grad. And we notice here, that it is the processes that are at fault. And when you are here you recognise that racism is there for all of us regardless of who our parents are. I call it the [UK1] bubble. You're part of it, but you're not part of it. So you naturally navigate to students who look like you – who are like you – they may have had different opportunities but they still are able to understand how that toxic racism in a place like this works.

Andrew and Daphne described a continuous process in which the recruitment of students was simultaneously founded on an evidentially meritocratic set of metrics, and also a nebulous set of judgements that happen behind closed doors. The visible rewarding of high-flying students with the best A Level results or first-class honours from the most demanding universities provided a smokescreen for decisions that advantaged white students.

White Performativity

One area of significant contention identified by less affluent students of colour at US1 and US2, was that their more affluent peers often adopted a range of white characteristics. In particular they suggested this was associated with holding a colour-blind perspective that limited their willingness to recognise racism within universities. We found that significant differences in wealth between students were used as a divisive mechanism by some students of colour to separate them from poorer, less wealthy students of colour. As discussed earlier some wealthier students of colour identified characteristics shared with wealthy white students as more sig-nificant than those shared with students of colour generally in terms of their identity as graduate students at an elite university. Typically this included shared experiences including prior education, parental occupation and access to wealth; and it materi-alised as shared forms of social activity and behaviour. In these accounts there was a feeling of the *naturalness* of friendship groups and behaviours that aligned within a context of whiteness. Judith Butler discusses how individual acts such as gestures, habits and speech determine our subjectivity, this shows that we can use performativity to understand how identities are marked out through a process of enactment (Butler, 1990b; 1990b). Such performativity resonates with the practice and repetition of behaviours throughout an individuals' life history, becoming ingrained within the body as *habitus;* they are both the materialisation of the structure itself and a means by which the structure regulates itself (Bourdieu, 1984). It was noticeable that more affluent students, unlike less affluent peers, often provided colour-blind accounts of race in elite universities. Warren argues that 'Color-blindness as a performative of white privilege functions as naming, a repetitious elision of power differentials that cites the discursive power of meritocracy – the myth that colour has not historical legacy of racial inequality' (2001: 100, see also Butler, 1993). A process of colour-blindness means that whiteness is performed in such a way to protect the privileged status of whiteness it is, 'a strategic rhetoric or systemic process of oppression, looks to the individual and in effect, works to keep the system unchallenged' (Warren, 2001: 102). Affluent students of colour at US1 and US2 drew on their wealth, background, taste, dress and linguistic style to 'perform' whiteness with their white peers. This was recognised by working class, less affluent students of colour. Lorna a Korean student at US1 said,

> I see some of the Black students who want to be part of the same group as the white students, they want to be like them because they have access to all sorts of different privileges. So because some of them have come from similar backgrounds, they are friends with them and you can see how similar they are. They do the same sports, they go out together, they have the same tastes and they even dress the same. It is a way they know they can belong if they are part of that group.

In Lorna's account, the performance of whiteness was directly associated with physical and material characteristics. Whiteness was identified not simply with skin colour but with a whole range of embodied characteristics and shared activities. It was a way of belonging as much as it was a phenotypical, biological materialisation of skin tone. For more affluent students of colour, whiteness was part of the attributes they understood were normal and legitimate to succeed within an elite university. This comfort in deploying aspects of whiteness also materialised within narrative accounts of their understandings of the significance of race and racism in their universities. Sarah, a Latina student at US1 noted similar characteristics to those described by Lorna; but she also relayed this to how these students were politically positioned,

> I see some of the African American students who are not part of the student activism which pushes for students of colour to be seen as part of the real student body here. They are not active in this way, they get on with their

work and for them that's what it's about and they have friends who are white and if you did not see them but heard them you could not tell what their ethnicity is. Some of my peers who are students of colour do this because they want to be accepted.

For students like Tom, who was not engaged in political activism, his colour-blind narrative provided a solid explanation for his choices and experiences as a US2 graduate student,

> I don't see it as being about race, I don't see race in that way. My friends are my friends because of who they are and because we get on. There are lots of things we have in common – things that we share and do together – it's about that rather than the fact that they are white and I am Black.

More affluent students of colour, such as Tom, appeared to deploy white forms of social and cultural capital because it was engrained within their life histories. They readily identified with the forms of whiteness that were embedded within structures and systems of elite university because this was knowledge they were comfortable with. It was knowledge that had been at the heart of their entire educational journeys. By doing so, they often did not fail to recognise broader patterns of racial inequality, they simply recognised it as not being a factor in their own experience. By framing their personal experience within a colour-blind perspective they were able to justify their own recognition of the higher value placed on white, middle-class forms of capitals. They were able to recognise and benefit from the dynamics of whiteness within an elite university without needing to express concerns about the racism underpinning whiteness.

Conclusions

The most significant finding to emerge between all the students in our research was the distinct differences in individuals' sense of belonging. These were clearly often shaped by multiple different factors that included past educational opportunities, family circumstances, geography, chance and luck. However, unsurprisingly race and class were often closely associated with all of these and other factors that determined different outcomes. Whiteness, as both a phenotypical marker of identity but also a visible marker of types of behaviour, beliefs and attitudes was a consistent feature of the elite university. White forms of capitals, which again materialise as a range of characteristics, behaviours, attitudes and beliefs are heavily weighted as the best, most effective forms of capital. Graduate students at elite universities were in essence engaged in a competition for white capitals. Many students of colour were disadvantaged in that competition because they did not bring pre-existing white capitals to the university; they were effectively handicapped by having access to less or less effective capitals within the elite university. This positioning, as lesser players in the competition often seemed directly correlated to feelings of discomfort and not belonging. It also appeared to be a regulatory practice particularly in the context of social shifts in opinion about inequality. Elite universities regulate the reproduction of whiteness. Students who do not possess white capitals are disadvantaged in comparison to those who possess more or better forms of white capital. Simultaneously a narrative of elite university meritocracy ensures that those students with greater access to white capitals, and who are continuously advantaged by these throughout their educational journeys, are imbued with the knowledge they are engaged in an equitable competition. They do not doubt the legitimacy of their personal success within a competition that rewards their personal advantageous characteristics.

Notes

1   The full semantic and social origins of 'chav' are obscure, but it is partly linked to the Romany languages of Gypsy and Roma ethnic groups who are themselves problematically identified as highly marginalised white community not accorded the same privileges as other white groups (Bhopal and Myers, 2008).
2   'comp' refers to a Comprehensive School in the UK. These are non-selective, publicly funded, secondary schools.
3   Black, Asian and minority ethnic (BAME) is a term used to describe people of colour in the UK.
4   Advanced level exams (A Levels) are compulsory exams taken at age 18 in the UK and are usually required for entrance to university.

9

CONCLUSIONS

Recognising the Unequal Field of Elite Universities

In many respects, the physical spaces of elite universities disguise the extent of their economic and cultural power. The most elite universities, those branded the 'Global super-league' by *The Economist* (2005), are associated with very localised identities. As discussed in Chapter 7 these local identities draw heavily from the histories, geography and physical spaces of specific locations to impart meaning within elite university brands. In Oxford and Cambridge in the UK and Cambridge, Massachusetts in the US the geographical name itself is associated with the university field. Elsewhere the resonance of a Columbia or Brown, Princeton or Yale are recognisable beyond the narrow field of academia alone. These local identities are associated with individual institutional identities but also signify the shared characteristics of elite universities within their competitive fields. In this final chapter we consider the relationship between these shared characteristics, their materialisation in the form of elite universities and the apparent instinctive drive of elite universities to reproduce noticeable inequalities.

Recognisability

Although it is problematic to provide an empirical measurement of the recognisability of a university name or brand, recognisability is a key metric for measuring institutional status and standing within the competitive field of higher education. It sits alongside other metrics such as standings in global and national rankings that in principle are more readily quantified (see Brankovic, 2022). The nature of such rankings means that their respective purveyors often work tirelessly to highlight distinctions between themselves; consequently exact measurements of research impact or teaching quality often vary between rankings. There also remains an underlying suspicion that at times, rankings provided for specific audiences are tailored around

DOI: 10.4324/9781003029922-9

the domestic or global audiences the ranking provider hopes to attract. *The Guardian* newspaper, for example produces an annual ranking of UK universities that often includes unexpected anomalies in the standing of the UK universities. Whilst these anomalies might simply reflect an objective attempt at constructing accurate metrics; more cynically it might be suggested the metrics are driven in some degree by the need to generate headlines, readership and advertising income.

Similarly, recognisability is the sense of shared attributes and characteristics amongst distinctive groupings of institutions. In the UK, more nebulous nomenclature such as red-brick or plate-glass universities have tended to be superseded by more clearly defined sector groupings. Some of these are based on specific, and often exclusive, membership criteria such as the Russell Group or Million+ group. Other terminologies such as post-1992 universities reflect specific types of institution. In the US there are well-defined groupings such as the Ivy League and other less clear-cut groups such as the Public Ivies.

Beyond institutional measures of status, individual academics are also measured and ranked. The increasing prevalence and accessibility of individual citations scores provided through *Google Scholar* or *Scopus* aligned with impact rankings for journals such as *Scimago* all provide means to amalgamate data on individual academic output that feeds into the metrics of institutional rankings. It also positions academics in relation to each other. It is free and only takes a few minutes to register for a personal *Google Scholar* account. By doing so, academics make public metrics including a total number of citations and H-Index[1] that facilitate making direct comparisons between different academics.

Taken together the measures of recognisability, institutional and individual metrics indicate that universities are overtly competitive fields. The competition for status, standing and recognisability is both continuous and etched into all aspects of the university; it is played institutionally and by individual social actors. In essence, it clearly resembles Bourdieu's (1996) and Bourdieu and Wacquant (1992) descriptions of a competitive field in which individual actors compete for resources in the form of economic, social and cultural capitals. In our research this was evidenced in graduate students recognition of the competitive field of their elite universities. They also highlighted the relational forces they brought to bear upon that competition, including their own prior access to different capitals and their personal learned and practised characteristics and traits, their habitus. Their complicity within these processes was readily signalled by their recognition of the competition and their decisions not to withdraw from the competition. So even those students who most readily identified structural inequality within elite universities still persisted with their studies.

The recognition of eliteness associated with all aspects of elite universities is the clearest indicator that their status and standing are legitimised beyond the domestic or national field. They are readily understandable as global phenomena. Again this was recognised by the graduate students we spoke to. Some described their own highly mobile pasts reflecting family backgrounds that can be understood in terms of global elites. Many more identified the potential for their own futures to be lived on a global stage. Ironically however, as discussed in Chapter 7, the brands of elite universities maintained clearly defined local origins, often wedded to relatively small geographical locations. In many respects the brands of elite universities are one conduit by which the local cultural capital of elite universities is imposed upon global economies. This local:global relationship has greater potency than similar products with brands tied to local geographies. Champagne, Scotch Whisky and Prosciutto Crudo, for example are subjected to European Union law prohibiting production outside of clearly delineated territory. This undoubtably recognises the potency of these as global products and protects brands by maintaining the quality and scarcity of these products. Elite university brands fulfil the same functions but also go much further. They are both self-regulating functions of their own institutional value and also of the wider field of global higher education. The potency of brands such as Oxford or Cambridge, Harvard or Yale, is that their role as producers of knowledge maps across higher education to validate and differentiate the entire field.

We have described elite university brands as cosmopolitan brands (Myers and Bhopal, 2021) to highlight the significance of the local:global relationship between elite universities. We understand cosmopolitan brands as a means by which elite universities extend and consolidate their own power bases by deploying cultural capital in the form of knowledge production. This is a process that also reflects Bourdieu's account of the extension of domestic power within neo-liberal, global economies (1998a; 2005). By doing so, the links between elite universities and other elite groups, particularly those in politics and the media become apparent. Cosmopolitan brands are one means by which the structural processes of elite universities maintain the institutional position and the standing of the social actors within their field. Inherent inequalities of race and class in society generally are regulated and transmitted generationally within the brand. The roots and routes of cosmopolitanism are historically long established and broadly distributed within different intellectual traditions. Sometimes they are simplified within a 'ground-setting fable' (Inglis, 2012: 12) that links ancient Greek stoics, possibly by way of St Paul and early Christianity (Derrida, 2001); Kant's *ius cosmopoliticum* as the Enlightenment staging post for rethinking social and political responses to the holocaust and more recent accounts of globalisation (Inglis, 2012). As a feature of globalisation in late modernity, cosmopolitanism locates the local characteristics of university brands within their participation in global higher education economies. This can be understood within Beck's account of a 'Second Age of Modernity' underpinned by cosmopolitanism and characterised as the decreasing significance of national borders, and increasingly non-territorial economies in which capital and labour become more mobile (Beck, 2006). Such characteristic understandings of global economies were often described by our participants who recognised their engagement within universities that positioned them to take advantage of global employment opportunities in the future (including future employment as academics within elite universities). Ironically, the emergence of economies unconstrained by national interests does not decrease the value of the local brand; if anything, the value still associated with locality is a useful indicator of a brand's scarcity value. Again, the comparison can be made with geographically specific food production: Despite the mass production of quality sparkling wines across all wine-producing regions, the cachet of Champagne retains greater economic value.

For Beck, these trends have the potential to address social injustice within nation states. His work on the cosmopolitan emerges out of inter-disciplinary discourse that, 'foreground the ethical settlement of the good society in contexts of global flows of people, capital and values' (Keith, 2006: 3). He anticipates individualised reflexive identities emerging to challenge the status quo, for example or reimagines mobilities as a means of migration engendering 'world (societal) upward mobility' (Beck, 2006: 149). In our research, it often appeared that the cosmopolitan nature of universities and their brands were designed to forestall the potential for addressing structural inequalities. Instead, the brand was a significant contributing element to maintaining the *status quo*. Its value in producing globally mobile individuals was an exclusive function that tended to self-select individuals who already had access to greater mobility. Mobility and access to global economies for these individuals were associated with their own agency and ability to shape their lives; in distinction to flows of refugees or displaced communities who do not share a similar investment in the benefits of mobility.

Throughout our research, we identified patterns of inequality around race and class that often appeared well-understood as unacceptable features of elite university life. The same inequalities were concurrently identified across a range of political and media discourses. The ability of elite universities to navigate a path through the concerns raised about their inherent racism and classism, *without significantly changing their inequitable outcomes*, is in part determined by the recognisability of their status. For graduate students, including those subject to inequitable outcomes, their experience is framed by recognition of the value of the credentials they will acquire. The institution itself recognises its own ability, as a producer of knowledge recognised globally as the most valid, to regulate or confirm or deny accusations of inequity. There are also institutions inexorably connected through generations of past elite students and academics, now in positions of power and capable of influencing media and political agendas. The self-regulatory function of elite universities is a reflection of elites more generally. In Bourdieu's (1977; 1996) terms, elite universities shape the doxa, the commonly held beliefs about what is natural and unchallengeable in the world. The inequities of elite universities are essentially granted a status of expected, normal, business as usual.

Race/Racism in an Elite Field

The two most significant forms of inequality that emerged in our discussions with graduate students were those of race and class. Inevitably Bourdieu's (1984; 1986) work on social structure and his key analytical tools of field, capitals and habitus provide a clear means of understanding class differences. Bourdieu's detailed analysis of the conditions that reproduce social inequality and preserve the status of elite groups have however often been a problematic area for researchers interested in race, racism and ethnicity. This is largely because there are few direct references to any of these topics in his own research. Bourdieu's early ethnographic work in Algeria presents his most direct account of race, ethnicity and colonialism, however, 'the concepts of habitus, field, capital and practice do not appear as integral aspects' (Loyal, 2009: 408) in this work. Loyal (2009) cautions against over-playing the Algerian research but argues Bourdieu's does contribute to sociological understandings of race and ethnicity, and that such insights fall within the scope of his wider project. Identifying a broader trend towards the rediscovery and discussion of Bourdieu's work on colonialism, Go (2013) argues this is rarely understood in terms of the production of a systematic theorising of colonialisation. If, Bourdieu's *sociology of colonialism eludes us*' (Go, 2013: 50), this, according to Go, does Bourdieu an injustice and he argues the 'seeds' for concepts such as habitus and field are all identifiable as '*originating in a critique of colonialism*' (Go, 2013: 51) despite not being explicitly named.

Few of the graduate students in our research had direct experience of being colonial subjects, though some were generationally close to parents or grandparents with such experiences. More generally, students recognised colonialism as a significant shaping factor within global politics and also specifically in relation to the field of elite universities. Our research was conducted against a backdrop of progressive student political discourse in which elite, and non-elite, universities were being challenged for their ongoing failures to address racial inequality. This included calls in both the US and the UK for institutions to disavow and apologise for historic links to the slave trade. Universities were also being increasingly critiqued for adopting a white, Western-centric curriculum that ignores knowledge produced outside of Europe and the US, and also, by more marginal communities in the west. This discourse, in the UK in particular, was also taking place against the backdrop of increasing numbers of student recruitment. Consequently, there were a significant number of students in our research (reflecting broader university demographics more generally), who were *first generation students*; whose parents had not previously attended university and who tended to be students of colour and those from less affluent, working-class backgrounds. To understand these students' experiences Bourdieu's account of colonial identities, particularly colonial identities shaped by changing economic structure, provides a useful means of positioning race and racism as regulating factors within institutional structures.

Bourdieu's (1962) account of peasants' adeptness when playing within the rules and practices of traditional village economies but out of their depth, when confronted with urban market economies is an early depiction of the significance of habitus. Go (2013) suggests that the habitus displayed by Algerian peasants is inevitably a colonial identity. It is a habitus shaped by colonial structures and embedded within the bodies of Algerian peasants; for Bourdieu these engrained dispositions undermine Fanon's advocacy for a peasant revolution in Algeria in *A Dying Coloni-alism* (Fanon, 1965). The potentials of a revolution limited because,

> the peasant's being is above all a certain *manner* of being, a habitus, a per-manent and general disposition before the world and others, he can remain a peasant even when he no longer has the possibility of behaving like one.
> *(Bourdieu and Sayad, 2015: 101)*

For graduate students unaccustomed to the field of elite universities, the habitus they bring to the university is that of a non-elite other. Not only do they experi-ence the feelings of discomfort associated with being in an environment in which they do not belong but they also recognise they are not positioned to actively chal-lenge the institution. The practised dispositions of their lives prior to attending an elite university include an immersion within the *doxa* legitimising elite universities as unchallengeable. At the same time, their presence within that field is deeply problematic for other social actors who do feel at home and do belong because of their more privileged backgrounds.

The recognition of who belongs and who does not belong, of who is com-fortable and who is uncomfortable, is both a symptom of the conditions of being a student at an elite university and also evidence of the processes by which the university adapts to change that threatens its *status quo*. So when it is suggested students of colour are privileged because they are *filling a quota*, this is working on multiple levels to maintain the privileged status of already privileged groups. First, it ensures that more privileged students, those whose habitus has been trained and practised and facilitated to ease their access to an elite university, are reassured of their greater value. These students understand elite universities meritocratic nar-ratives to validate their entitlement to an elite place is a direct recognition of their personal endeavours. Their perceived identities in which despite acknowledging their advantageous backgrounds, they still understand their own and others similar to themselves, as the recipients of a rightful entitlement to elite university status. If this is undermined by the increasing presence of students who do not mirror their facilitated access, it is helpful to assert a counter-narrative of quotas to maintain the illusion of meritocracy. Second, this is a discourse that fosters discomfort for some students. It actively produces the conditions in which some students question their entitlement to be at an elite university. By doing so, it is a strategy that undermines their work by creating an environment in which it is harder to flourish. Finally, it devalues the cultural capital produced by these students. It is a means to categorise their knowledge production and their academic credentials as less valuable.

Bourdieu and Wacquant (1992: 97) describe field in spatial terms to highlight its analytical function of relational behaviours,

> a field may be defined as a network, or a configuration, of objective relations between positions. These positions are objectively defined, in their existence and in the determinations they impose upon their occupants, agents or institutions,

by their present and potential situation (situs) in the structure of the distribution of species of power (or capital) whose possession commands access to the specific profits that are at stake in the field, as well as by their objective relation to other positions (domination, subordination, homology, etc.).

Go (2013) argues that the relational standing of different groups in Algeria, such as dominant and subordinated groups or Europeans and Algerians, is an implicit theorisation of colonialism by Bourdieu as a field. It is 'like a field in that it shapes actors and their actions . . . [and] . . . in the sense that it is replete with struggle and conflict' (Go, 2013: 64). Race and ethnicity are a key function of defining status and hierarchy within this field; White Europeans occupying dominant positions whilst Algerians occupy subordinate spaces. The relation between dominant elites and a broad swathe of non-elite subordinated others is endlessly reproduced through the competitive processes of a colonial field. The competition itself highly regulated through very specific and unalterable markers such as race and ethnicity; unlike a 'free market', the colonial economy imposes a strict restrictive bar on what a student of colour can or cannot achieve.

Within the elite university, race and ethnicity may not exercise the same definitive bar as a colonial field; they do however regulate outcomes. For students of colour, access to, and benefit from, the elite university field is subjected to a general regime of restrictions. The rules of the field are the everyday rules of racism and white supremacy. At different times they adapt to changing social, economic or political circumstances; but inherently the rules are always designed to advantage white students and academics in the field. Adaptations made within elite university fields often resemble Bell's (1980) theorising of interest convergence; change happens but only when it suits white interests. In the long term, elite universities reproduce mechanisms that reassert racism despite appearing to redress racist inequality. Bell (1992) also notes that racial equality legislation is often deployed to trump calls for affirmative action. More recently and throughout the timespan of our research, accusations of systemic or institutional racism within universities, and within elite universities in particular, have been commonplace in the media. These often appear to be so obviously well-founded and evidenced that some institutions in both the US and the UK have pro-actively appeared to embed new systems to ensure more students of colour are recruited. Bell (1980), citing the prior experience of *Brown v. Board of Education*, would undoubtedly call out much of this work as an example of interest convergence in which it is in the better interests of white institutions and their white agents to give some ground rather than simply resist change. Whilst giving the appearance of addressing systemic or institutional racism by recruiting greater numbers of students of colour, universities simultaneously ensured they maintained racial hierarchies.

Those adaptations made by universities to address racism can best be understood as,

measures, usually steeped in liberal self-congratulation, [that] tend to address only the most blatant kinds of discrimination but they often become

> enshrined as *contradiction-closing* cases, which are assumed to have resolved
> problems of racism, rendering further action unnecessary and excessive.
>
> *(Warmington, 2020: 23)*

Warmington (2020) describes how such '*contradiction-closing* cases' only emerge when, 'racist practices threaten to destabilise rather than secure elite power that it is in the self-interest of elites to address racism through legislation and policy' (2020: 23). The example of quotas for under-represented students can be viewed as the type of policy that shuts down debate about who gains access to elite universities by demonstrably signalling institutional action to address inequalities. However, in the longer term, quotas are reimagined as a means to denigrate the students they benefit. In the same vein, *decolonising the curriculum* emerges within institutional discourse to signal action; but in practice despite their resonance within liberal progressive language, are often nebulous, ill-defined and unmeasurable practice. Interest convergence and contradiction-closing cases are the practical means by which racism is maintained and should be viewed as evidence of racial realism.

Elite university brands also played a significant role in ensuring a narrative of anti-racism was given credence at the same time as racist practice was being reproduced. Bell's (1991; 1992) account of racial realism includes two interrelated elements, the permanence of racism despite linear progressions in civil rights, and, the significance of socio-economic positioning in identifying inequality and power that are useful means of understanding how race and racism can be maintained within the work of the brand. It is worth noting that the value of realism has been highlighted across much scholarship focused on addressing inequalities; including, Kynch and Sen's (1983) insistence on identifying realism within economic models including Bourdieu's (1962) use of empirical research to understand socio-economic change. Bell's insistence on realism to highlight and distinguish lived experience from abstract ideas and theory is mirrored in the accounts of graduate students of colour suggesting the value they derive from their respective elite universities is less than that available to white students. Brands clearly worked to exclude both students from poorer backgrounds and students of colour. Students from Black, working-class backgrounds were differently disadvantaged along intersectional axes.

The reality for students of colour was that they encountered elite universities engaging in practice that differentiates experience and outcomes based on racial inequalities; as well as along class lines. The brand defines the recognisable ethos of elite universities as white spaces in which white knowledge is produced; in this sense the historic and local character of many elite universities is indicative of their embeddedness within traditional white stereotypes and white histories. As discussed the privileged recognition of knowledge production by elite universities as superior to other knowledge production is almost unassailable because those universities are able to 'self-certify' their own recognisable status. In this respect university brands are distinct from many other types of brands; rather than requiring marketing directors to develop and promote brand visibility, elite universities are the means to confirm their own brand value. For universities in which racism is a permanent feature, the brand does not have to change. In effect the concerns of consumers of the brand are not required to be noticed if they wish to claim the university and its brand are racist, because the university has such significant cultural capital within the global field of higher education it can simply contradict any criticism by deploying the power of its brand.

Bourdieu also confronts the impact of colonialism on the consciousness of subordinated groups in an echo of 'double consciousness' (Du Bois, 1989; Fanon, 2008), describing Algerians identifying all Europeans as social superiors and simultaneously conflating their status with the role of authority figures (e.g. teachers, policemen or administrators), suggesting an overarching, dominant class 'indissolubly connected with the colonial situation' (Bourdieu, 1962: 160). For Algerians 'the social order was such that the experience of the relation to the boss or the superior was superimposed upon, and identified itself with, the experience of the relation to the European. As a consequence Algerians tended to play the role of the Arab-as-seen-by-the-Frenchman' (Bourdieu, 1962: 161). Du Bois's use of 'double consciousness' is framed in terms of the displaced histories of Black Americans, 'the sense of always looking at ones' self through the eyes of others, of measuring one's soul by the tape of a world that looks on in an amused contempt and pity' (Du Bois, 1989: 8) Bourdieu's Algerians are displaced internally by colonialism and by associated modernising economic policy. There is some alignment in the way Du Bois refers to 'sensation' and a 'sense of' 'double consciousness' and Bourdieu's understanding of habitus, the ingrained traits and characteristics embodied through experience. Bourdieu describes habitus as a 'double and obscure relation' shaped by field and, also, 'constituting the field as a meaningful world' (Bourdieu and Wacquant, 1992: 127). In the field of elite universities, habitus is inevitably informed by race and ethnicity, and this has a direct relation to the social construction of everyday racism.

Bourdieu's analysis of colonialism in Algeria is also a useful means of flagging up how the relational competitions within an elite university for power or capitals are unsurprisingly determined by student's race and ethnicity. The university economy is a competitive market in which individuals compete for power, status and capitals. For academics this might materialise in recognition of their intellectual expertise (high-profile publications, prizes or invitations to deliver keynote speeches); in acknowledgement of their standing in their field (appointments to prestigious positions within their professional bodies) or in financial rewards (entering the higher echelons of professorial pay scales). Such competition readily aligns with Bourdieu's descriptions of cultural, social and economic capitals. For students at elite universities there are similar competitive processes: good grades, social networks and the promise of highly paid employment in the future. Whilst an idealised account of universities might suggest these are open competitions within free-market economies; the evidence of who gains access to elite universities, who achieve the best outcomes and who goes on to the best jobs suggest otherwise. Our research was particularly attentive to the relational competition for capitals that

Bourdieu identifies as a means of understanding how class and race are key factors in the economies of elite universities. Attending an elite university for students of colour was often a new and novel experience that impacted upon their identity, however it remains a mitigating rather than revolutionary factor in their personal development. It is not an experience that displaces or revokes past experience; as Bourdieu suggests,

> Habitus changes constantly in response to new experiences. Dispositions are subject to a kind of permanent revision, but one which is never radical, because it works on the basis of the premises established in the previous state. They are characterized by a degree of constancy and variation.
>
> *(Bourdieu, 2000: 161)*

The Elite University

Our participants identified processes that perpetuated long-standing inequalities in terms of their initial means to access elite universities, their experience of attending the university and even in their ambitions for the future. It was apparent that for many students from different backgrounds the recognisability of value associated with elite universities outweighed wider concerns about institutional inequalities or their personal discomfort being a student. This is not to suggest that students were uncritical or disengaged from debate about the roles of their universities. Many were actively critical and engaged in struggles to create institutional change. The fields of elite universities are full of ambitious, intelligent people who recognise they are in multiple forms of competition with each other. That competitive space has real and measurable rewards in terms of the different forms of capitals it produces. In an insecure world the brand of an elite university on a doctoral certificate infers great value on the holder. In terms of economic capital it delivers measurably advantageous rewards in the salary scales offered its graduates. It is also a means by which social networks are built to channel the access to those well-rewarded positions across the global economy. Underpinning those outcomes however is the legitimising value of its knowledge production; its cultural capital is essentially unchallengeable. Elite universities are effectively positioned as the ultimate arbiters of which knowledge is the most valuable. In addition their ability to fulfil that role is embedded across the interests of multiple other fields. Politics, the media, business and organised religion are all fields dominated by their own elite social actors who occupy those positions in part because of their prior links to elite universities. Their own roles are validated and legitimised by their accession from elite universities to elite social positions.

Perhaps the most significant finding of our research was that inequalities within elite universities are performed in an overt fashion. These are not inequalities that are disguised or hidden away. They are fully in view. It is not a secret that elite universities are founded on the same inequalities that underpin all facets of society. There is a readily accessible body of data, collated on a regular basis that lays bare inequalities of race and social class. Individual institutions, including elite universities, stand out because of their long-standing failures to address these inequalities. In addition to which such data are regularly cited in the media highlighting the specific inequalities associated with elite universities. More generally educational outcomes are framed by similar inequalities that are equally well-documented. It is well known, for example that school outcomes are likely to be affected by geographic location, socio-economic class, race and ethnicity. It is equally well known that pupils attending private fee-paying schools are less likely to fail their exams and more likely to attend university. Beyond the field of education we can identify similar patterns in the employment market, in housing and health outcomes. Overt inequalities are always readily evidenced even if attempts to redress their impact seem consistently doomed to failure.

Despite the overt nature of inequalities within elite universities it is often the case that when evidence emerges that some groups are excluded this is portrayed as a new problematic finding rather than the normal state of affairs. There is an assumption that the evidence is unclear or difficult to prove. The narratives around inequalities at elite universities often stress universities facing up to their responsibilities as part of a slow, but inevitable progression towards a more equitable society. One indication this is not the case is apparent in the repetitions of media stories. In 2010, under the headline, 'Twenty-one Oxbridge colleges took no black students last year', *The Guardian* reported on the findings of Freedom of Information requests to individual colleges at the Universities of Oxford and Cambridge. The data provided by these colleges identified, 'that Oxford's social profile is 89% upper- and middle-class, while 87.6% of the Cambridge student body is drawn from the top three socioeconomic groups. The average for British universities is 64.5%, according to the admissions body Ucas' (Vasagar, 2010). A disturbing element of this particular story is that its main focus is not about class inequalities but rather about the exclusion of students on the basis of race and ethnicity and their poorer outcomes when they leave these universities. *The Guardian* went on to note that, 'One Oxford college, Merton, has admitted no black students in five years – and just three in the last decade. Eleven Oxford colleges and 10 Cambridge colleges made no offers to black students for the academic year beginning autumn 2009'. A decade later, beneath the following headline, 'Cambridge University's poor diversity record highlighted by report', *The Guardian* reported, 'One college did not offer a place to any black applicants between 2012 and 2016' (Quinn, 2018). According to *The Guardian*, 'Some Cambridge University colleges have admitted no black students or have accepted as few as one a year between 2012 and 2016' and meanwhile at the University of Oxford, 'more than one in four of its colleges failed to admit a single black British student each year between 2015 and 2017'.

Inequalities are overt, recognisable features of the elite university field. Evidence of these inequalities has always been in the public domain. They are not an unwanted by-product of accumulated historic mistakes and errors of judgement but rather an ongoing strategy to maintain the interests of academic and non-academic elites. Racism and class inequality are the normal anticipated outcomes because the interests of elite universities are primarily the interests of a white, middle-class elite. Bourdieu (2005) describes the taken-for-granted nature of social structures including their inherent inequalities. Elite universities are uniquely positioned to defend their entitlement to their status from challenge. They are able to exert a particular form of power as the arbiters of whose cultural capital holds the greatest value. Along with non-elite universities they are knowledge producers; they are engaged in the day-to-day activities of research that produce new forms of knowledge. But in addition to this, their ongoing status as the most highly regarded institutions, grants them the privilege of establishing which forms of knowledge should be understood to be the most significant. In the competitive fields of universities, they are playing with a heavily loaded hand of cards; their own accumulated cultural capital determining which work, which people and which institutions hold the most value. In this competitive venture they inevitably pursue strategies to protect their own interests. At the micro-level these include the interests of students who most comfortably align with the white middle-class interests of the institution. At the macro level elite universities are engaged in shaping global economies. They do this through the successful positioning of their own people within elite positions. They are also engaged in the competition that asserts particular national interests; those of western universities particularly in the US and the UK, rather than universities in the global south or developing world.

In conclusion, elite universities serve their own interests. Occasionally these interests might be mitigated or forced to adapt to changing social and economic conditions. In the final reckoning however, the interests of elite universities are largely unassailable. Despite being a nebulous concept, elite universities deploy their wealth and status, their brands and reputation to ensure that the *'elite'* in elite universities is retained. Their eliteness remains visible and readily recognised.

Note

1 H-Index is a means of measuring both the productivity and impact of academic outputs through citations. In principle it ensures the significance of a single highly cited piece of work is not privileged disproportionately in relation to an author's whole body of work. It provides a figure for the highest cited output that is matched by the same, or a greater number, of outputs similarly cited.

REFERENCES

Aaker, D. (1991) *Managing brand equity*. New York: The Free Press.

AdvanceHE. (2021) *Equality and higher education: Student statistical report*. London: AdvanceHE.

Ali-Choudhury, R., Bennett, R. and Savani, S. (2009) 'University marketing directors' views on the components of a university brand', *International Review on Public and Non-profit Marketing*, 6 (1): 11.

Allan, A. and Charles, C. (2014) 'Cosmo girls: Configurations of class and femininity in elite educational settings', *British Journal of Sociology of Education,* 35 (3): 333–352.

Althusser, L. (1971) 'Ideology and state apparatuses (Notes towards an investigation)', in *Lenin and philosophy and other essays*, pp. 171–174.

Andrews, K. (2020) 'The radical "Possibilities" of black studies', *The Black Scholar*, 50 (3): 17–28.

Apple, M. (1998) 'Foreword', in Kincheloe, J., Steinberg, S., Rodriguez, N. and Chennault, R. (eds.) *White Reign*. New York: St Martin's Griffin, pp. ix–xiii.

Atkinson, R. and Flint, J. (2001) 'Accessing hidden and hard to reach populations: Snowball research strategies', *Social Research Update*, 33 (1): 1–4.

Ball, S. J. (2003) 'The teacher's soul and the terrors of performativity', *Journal of Education Policy*, 18 (2): 215–228.

Ball, S. J. (2012) 'Performativity, commodification and commitment: An I-Spy guide to the neoliberal university', *British Journal of Educational Studies*, 60 (1): 17–28.

Ball, S. J. (2016) 'Neoliberal education? Confronting the slouching beast', *Policy Futures in Education*, 14 (8): 1046–1059.

Ball, S. and Nikita, D. (2014) 'The global middle class and school choice: A cosmopolitan sociology', *Sociology Zeitschrift fuer Erziehungswissenschaft*, 17: 81–93.

Baudrillard, J. (1993) *Symbolic exchange and death*. London: Sage.

Bauman, Z. (2000a) *Liquid modernity*. Cambridge: Polity.

Bauman, Z. (2000b) 'Tourists and vagabonds: Or, living in postmodern times', in Davis, J. E. (ed.) *Identity and social change*. New Jersey: Transaction Publishers.

Beck, U. (1992) *Risk society*. London: Sage.

Beck, U. (2002) 'The cosmopolitan society and its enemies', *Theory, Culture & Society*, 19 (1–2): 17–44.

Beck, U. (2006) 'The cosmopolitan state: Redefining power in the global age', *International Journal of Politics, Culture, and Society,* 18 (3–4): 143–159.

Beck, U., Bonss, W. and Lau, C. (2003) 'The theory of reflexive modernization: Problematic, hypotheses and research programme', *Theory, Culture & Society,* 20 (2): 1–33.

Bell, D. (1980) 'Brown v. Board of education and the interest-convergence dilemma', *Harvard Law Review,* 93 (3): 518–533.

Bell, D. (1991) 'Racial realism', *Connecticut Law Review,* 24 (2): 363–380.

Bell, D. (1992) *Faces at the bottom of the well: The permanence of racism.* New York: Basic Books.

Bhambra, G. K., Gebrial, D. and Nişancıoğlu, K. (2018) *Decolonising the university.* London: Pluto Press.

Bhopal, K. (2018) *White privilege: The myth of a post-racial society.* Bristol: Policy/Bristol University Press.

Bhopal, K. (2022) 'Academics of colour in elite universities in the UK and the USA: The "unspoken system of exclusion"', *Studies in Higher Education,* 47 (11): 2127–2137.

Bhopal, K. and Myers, M. (2008) *Insiders, outsiders and others: Gypsies and identity.* Hatfield: University of Hertfordshire Press.

Bhopal, K. and Myers, M. (forthcoming, 2022) *Routes through higher education: Race, class and gender.* London: Routledge.

Bhopal, K., Myers, M. and Pitkin, C. (2020) 'Routes through higher education: BME students and the development of a 'specialisation of consciousness'', *British Educational Research Journal,* 46 (6): 1321–1337.

Binder, A., Davis, D. and Bloom, N. (2016) 'Career funnelling: How elite students learn to define and desire 'prestigious' jobs', *Sociology of Education,* 89 (1): 20–39.

Boden, R., Kenway, J. and James, M. (2020) 'Private schools and tax advantage in England and Wales—The Longue Duree', *Critical Studies in Education,* 63 (3): 291–306.

Bol, T. and Weeden, K. (2015) 'Occupational closure and wage inequality in Germany and the United Kingdom', *European Sociological Review,* 31 (3): 354–369.

Boliver, V. (2013) 'How fair is access to more prestigious universities?' *British Journal of Sociology of Education,* 64 (2): 344–364.

Boliver, V. (2016) 'Exploring ethnic inequalities in admission to Russell Group universities', *Sociology,* 50 (2): 246–266.

Bonilla-Silva, E. (2002) 'The linguistics of colour-blind racism: How to talk nasty about blacks without sounding "racist"', *Critical Sociology,* 28 (1–2): 41–64.

Bonilla-Silva, E. (2006) *Racism without racists: Colour-blind racism and the persistence of racial inequality in the United States.* Lanham, MD: Rowman and Littlefield Publishers.

Bourdieu, P. (1962) *The Algerians.* Beacon Press.

Bourdieu, P. (1977) *Outline of a theory of practice* (Vol. 16). Cambridge: Cambridge University Press.

Bourdieu, P. (1984) *Distinction: A social critique of the judgement of taste.* Cambridge, MA: Harvard University Press.

Bourdieu, P. (1985) 'The social space and the genesis of groups', *Information (International Social Science Council),* 24 (2): 195–220.

Bourdieu, P. (1986) 'The forms of capital', in Richardson, J. (ed.) *Handbook of theory and research for the sociology of education.* Westport, CT: Greenwood, pp. 241–258.

Bourdieu, P. (1988) *Homo academicus.* Cambridge: Polity.

Bourdieu, P. (1989) 'Social space and symbolic power', *Sociological Theory,* 7 (1): 14–25.

Bourdieu, P. (1993a) *Sociology in question* (Vol. 18). London: Sage.

Bourdieu, P. (1993b) *The field of cultural reproduction.* Oxford: Polity.

Bourdieu, P. (1996) *The state nobility.* Oxford: Polity.

Bourdieu, P. (1998a) *Acts of resistance: Against the tyranny of the market*. New York: New Press.

Bourdieu, P. (1998b) *Practical reason: On the theory of action*. Stanford: Stanford University Press.

Bourdieu, P. (2000) *Pascalian meditations*. Stanford: Stanford University Press.

Bourdieu, P. (2005) *The social structures of the economy*. Cambridge: Polity.

Bourdieu, P. (2008) *Sketches for a self-analysis*. Cambridge: Polity.

Bourdieu, P. and Passeron, J. (1964/1979) *The inheritors: French students and their relation to culture*. Chicago, IL: Chicago University Press.

Bourdieu, P. and Passeron, J. (1977) *Reproduction in education, society and culture*. London: Sage.

Bourdieu, P. and Passeron, J. (1990) *Reproduction in education, society and culture* (Vol. 4). London: Sage.

Bourdieu, P. and Sayad, A. (2015) *Uprooting*. Cambridge: Cambridge University Press.

Bourdieu, P. and Wacquant, L. (1992) *An invitation to reflexive sociology*. Chicago: University of Chicago Press.

Bowles, S. and Gintis, H. (2011) *Schooling in Capitalist America: Educational reform and the contradictions of economic life*. Chicago: Haymarket Books.

Brankovic, J. (2022) 'Why rankings appear natural (But aren't)', *Business and Society*, 6 (4): 801–806.

Braun, V. and Clarke, V. (2006) 'Using thematic analysis in psychology', *Qualitative Research in Psychology*, 3 (2): 77–101.

Bray, M. and Lykins, C. (2012) *Shadow education: Private supplementary tutoring and its implications for policy makers in Asia, Philippines*. Hong Kong: Comparative Education Research Centre.

Burrow, G. (2008) *A history of Yale's school of medicine*. New Haven: Yale University Press.

Butler, J. (1990a) *Gender trouble: Feminism, and the subversion of identity*. New York: Routledge.

Butler, J. (1990b) 'Performative acts and gender constitution: An essay in phenomenology and feminist theory', in Case, S. (ed.) *Performing feminisms: Feminist critical theory and theatre*. Baltimore, MD: Johns Hopkins University Press, pp. 198–209.

Butler, J. (1993) *Bodies that matter: On the discursive limits of 'Sex'*. New York: Routledge.

Cabrera, N. (2014) 'Exposing whiteness in higher education: White male college students minimising racism, claiming victimization and recreating white supremacy', *Race, Ethnicity and Education*, 17 (1): 30–55.

Calhoun, C. (2003) 'Pierre Bourdieu', in Ritzer, G. (ed.) *The Blackwell companion to major contemporary social theorists*. Oxford: Blackwell Publishing, pp. 274–309.

Carter, P. (2003) ' "Black" cultural capital, status positioning and schooling conflicts for low-income African American Youth', *Social Problems*, 50 (1): 136–155.

Carter, P. (2005) *Keepin' it real: School success beyond black and white*. New York: Oxford University Press.

Chakrabarty, N., Roberts, L. and Preston, J. (eds.) (2016) *Critical race theory in England*. London and New York: Routledge.

Chapman, T. and Bhopal, K. (2013) 'Countering common sense understandings of 'good parenting:' Women of color advocating policy change for their children. [in special issue:' Honoring Derrick Bell's Contributions to Teacher Education, Race, Poverty and Leadership',]', *Race Ethnicity and Education*, 16 (4): 562–586.

Charles, C., Dinwiddie, G. and Massey, D. (2004) 'The continuing consequences of segregation: Family stress and college academic performance', *Social Science Quarterly*, 85 (5): 1353–1373.

Coleman, J. (1988) 'Social capital in the creation of human capital', *American Journal of Sociology*, 92: S95–120.

Connell, R., Ashenden, D., Kessler, S. and Dowsett, G. (1982) *Making the difference: Schools, families and social divisions in society.* Sydney: Allen and Unwin.

Cookson, P. W. and Persell, C. H. (1985) *Preparing for power: America's elite boarding schools.* Basic Books.

Cookson, P and Persell, C. (2010) 'Preparing for power: Twenty-five years later', in Howard, A. and Gaztambide-Fernandez, R. (eds.) *Educating elites: Class, privilege and educational advantage.* Lanham: Rowman and Littlefield, pp. 13–30.

Courtois, A. (2015) 'Thousands waiting at our gates: Moral character, legitimacy and social justice in Irish elite schools', *British Journal of Sociology of Education*, 36 (1): 53–70.

Courtois, A. (2017) *Elite schooling and social inequality: Privilege and power in Ireland's top private schools.* Springer.

Crenshaw, K. (1991) 'Mapping the margins: Intersectionality, identity politics and violence against women of color', *Stanford Law Review*, 43 (5): 1253–1351.

Crenshaw, K. W., Gotanda, N., Peller, G. and Thomas, K. (eds.) (1995) *Critical race theory: The key writings that formed the movement.* New York: The New Press.

Cribb, J., Sibieta, L. and Vignoles, A. (2013) *Entry into grammar schools in England.* Institute for Fiscal Studies.

Crul, M., Keskiner, E. and Lelie, F. (2017) 'The upcoming new elite among children of immigrants: A cross country and cross sector comparison', *Ethnic and Racial Studies*, 40 (2): 209–229.

Cullinane, C. (2017) *Life lessons.* London: Sutton Trust.

Delgado, R. and Stefancic, J. (2000) *Critical race theory: The cutting edge.* Philadelphia, PA: Temple University Press.

Delgado, R. and Stefancic, J. (2017) *Critical race theory: An introduction.* 3rd edn. New York: New York University Press.

Derrida, J. (2001) *On cosmopolitanism and forgiveness.* London: Routledge.

DfE. (2012) *Government publishes destination data for the first time.* www.gov.uk/government/news/government-publishes-destination-data-for-the-first-time (Accessed: 13.04.21).

DfE (Department for Education). (2020) *The earnings returns to postgraduate degrees in the UK Research report September 2020.* London: DfE.

Du Bois, W. E. B. (1989) *The souls of black folks.* New York: Bantam.

Duggan, A. (2016) 'Reactionaries and revolutionaries: Classical fairy tales and class', *Culture Matters,* www.culturematters.org.uk/index.php/arts/fiction/item/2327-reactionaries-and-revolutionaries-classical-fairy-tales-and-class (Accessed: 12.04.21).

Dundes, A. (ed.) (1988) *Cinderella, a case book* (Vol. 3). University of Wisconsin Press.

Durkheim, E. (2014) *The rules of sociological method: And selected texts on sociology and its method.* Simon and Schuster.

Dyer, R. (1988) 'White', *Screen*, 29 (4): 44–64.

Dyer, R. (1997) *White.* New York: Routledge.

Eastwood, D. (2012) 'Global tunes and national melodies: Being global and sounding local', in *The globalization of higher education.* London: Palgrave Macmillan, pp. 34–39.

The Economist. 2005. *The brains business*, September 8.

EHRC (Equalities and Human Rights Commission). (2019) *Tackling racial harassment: Universities challenged.* London: EHRC.

Elliott, A. and Urry, J. (2010) *Mobile lives.* London: Routledge.

Elliot Major, L. and Machin, S. (2018) *Social mobility and its enemies.* London: Penguin Random House.

Epstein, D. (2014) 'Race-ing class ladies: Lineages of privilege in an elite South African School', *Globalisation, Societies and Education*, Special Issue *Elite Schools in Globalising Circumstances*, 12 (2): 228–243.

Fahey, J. (2014) 'Privileged girls: The place of feminism and feminism in place', *Globalisation, Societies and Education*, Special Issue *Elite Schools in Globalising Circumstances*, 12 (2): 228–243.

Fanon, F. (1965) *A dying colonialism.* Trans. Haakon Chevalier. New York: Grove Press.

Fanon, F. (2008) *Black skin, white masks.* London: Pluto Press.

Feagin, J. (2013) *Systemic racism: A theory of oppression.* New York: Routledge.

Feagin, J. R. and Barnett, B. M. (2004) 'Success and failure: How systemic racism trumped the Brown v. Board of Education decision', *University of Illinois Law Review*, 2004 (5): 1099–1130.

Feagin, J. R., Vera, H. and Imani, N. (2014). *The agony of education: Black students at a White university.* New York: Routledge.

Findlay, A, King, R. and Smith, F. (2012) 'World class? An investigation of globalisation, difference and international student mobility', *Transactions of the Institute of British Geographers*, 37: 118–31.

Flick, U. (1998) *An introduction to qualitative research.* London: Sage.

Forbes, J. and Lingard, B. (2013) 'Elite school capitals and girls' schooling: Understanding the (re)production of privilege through a habitus of assuredness', in Maxwell, C. and Aggleton, P. (eds.) *Privilege, agency and affect.* Basingstoke: Palgrave Macmillan, pp. 50–68.

Forbes, J. and Lingard, B. (2015) 'Assured optimism in a Scottish Girls' school: Habitus and the (Re)production of Global Privilege', *British Journal of Sociology of Education*, 36 (1): 116–136.

Foucault, M. (1973) *The birth of the clinic: An archaeology of medical perception.* London: Tavistock.

Foucault, M. (1977) *Discipline and punish: The birth of the prison.* London: Allen Lane.

Frankenberg, R. (1993) *White women, race matters: The social construction of race.* Minneapolis: University of Minnesota Press.

Freyne, P. (2021) Harry and Meghan: The union of two great houses, the Windsors and the Celebrities, is complete. *The Irish Times*, 8 March 2021. https://www.irishtimes.com/culture/tv-radio-web/harry-and-meghan-the-union-of-two-great-houses-the-windsors-and-the-celebrities-is-complete-1.4504502

Friedman, H. (2013) *Playing to win: Raising children in a competitive culture.* Berkeley: University of California Press.

Friedman, J. (2017) 'Everyday nationalism and elite research universities in the USA and England', *Higher Education*, 1–15.

Giddens, A. (1984) *The constitution of society: Outline of the theory of structuration.* California: University of California Press.

Gillborn, D. (2005) 'Education as an Act of White Supremacy: Whiteness, critical race theory and education reform', *Journal of Education Policy*, 20 (4): 485–505.

Gillborn, D. (2008) *Racism and education: Coincidence or conspiracy?* New York: Routledge.

Gillborn, D. (2012) 'The white working class, racism and respectability: Victims, degenerates and interest-convergence', in Bhopal, K. and Preston, J. (eds.) *Intersectionality and race in education.* London: Routledge, pp. 37–64.

Gillborn, D. (2018) 'Heads I win, tails you lose: Anti-Black racism as fluid, relentless, individual and systemic', *Peabody Journal of Education*, 93 (1): 66–77.

Gillborn, D., Bhopal, K., Crawford, C., Demack, S., Gholami, R., Kitching, K., Kiwan, D. and Warmington, P. (2021) *Evidence for the commission on racial and ethnic disparities.* Birmingham: University of Birmingham.

Gillborn, D., Rollock, N., Vincent, C. and Ball, S. (2012) 'You got a pass, so what more do you want'? Race, class and gender intersections in the educational experiences of the black middle class', *Race, Ethnicity and Education*, 15 (1): 121–139.

Giroux, H. (1997) 'Racial politics and the pedagogy of whiteness', in Hill, M. (ed.) *Whiteness: A critical reader*. New York: New York University Press, pp. 294–315.

Goffman, E. (1951) 'Symbols of class status', *The British Journal of Sociology*, 2 (4): 294–304.

Goffman, E. (1998) 'A vague but suggestive concept: The total social fact', in James, W. and Allen, A. (eds.) *Marcel Maus: A centenary tribute*. New York: Berghahn Books.

Gove, M. (2013) The Progressive Betrayal. Speech delivered to the social market foundation 5 February 2013. www.mixcloud.com/SMFthinktank/michael-gove-speaks-to-the-smf-on-the-progressive-betrayal/ (Accessed: 30.12.21).

Green, F. and Kynaston, D. (2019) *Engines of privilege: Britain's private school problem*. London: Bloomsbury.

Green, F., Anders, J., Henderson, M. and Henseke, G. (2017) *Who chooses private schooling in Britain and why?* London, Centre for Research on Learning and Life Chances (LLAKES), Research Paper 62.

Greenhalgh-Spencer, H. (2015) 'Social class as flow and mutability: The Barbados case', *British Journal of Sociology of Education*, 36 (1): 156–173.

Griffiths, P., Glossop, M., Powis, B. and Strang, J. (1993) 'Reaching hidden populations of drug users by privileged access interviewers: Methodological and practical issues', *Addiction*, 88: 1617–1636.

Halfon, R. (2021) *The Forgotten: How white working class pupils have been let down and how to change it*. London: House of Commons Education Select Committee, First report of session 2021–2022.

Hart, S. (1998) 'The future for brands', in Hart, S. and Murphy, J. (eds.) *Brands*. Basingstoke: MacMillan.

Hartigan, Jr, J. (1997) 'Name calling', in Wray, M. and Newitz, A. (eds.) *White trash: Race and class in American*. New York: Routledge, pp. 41–56.

Hartocollis, A. (2020) 'The affirmative action battle at Harvard is not over', *New York Times*, 18 February. www.nytimes.com/2020/02/18/us/affirmative-action-harvard.html.

Hartocollis, A. (2021) 'After a year of turmoil, elite universities welcome more freshman classes' *New York Times* www.nytimes.com/2021/04/17/us/minority-acceptance-ivy-league-cornell.html.

Harvey, C. and Maclean, M. (2008) 'Capital theory and the dynamics of elite business networks in Britain and France', *The Sociological Review*, 56 (1): 103–120.

Henfield, M., Moore, J. and Wood, C. (2008) 'Inside and outside gifted education programming: Hidden challenges for African American students', *Exceptional Children*, 74 (4): 433–450.

Holmes, S. (2004) 'All you've got to worry about is the task, having a cup of tea, and doing a bit of sunbathing', in Holmes, S. and Jermyn, D. (eds.) *Understanding reality television*. London: Psychology Press.

Hooks, B. (1997) 'Representing whiteness in the black imagination', in Frankenberg, R. (ed.) *Displacing whiteness*. Durham, NC: Duke University Press, pp. 165–179.

Horvat, E. (2003) 'The Interactive Effects of Race and Class in Educational Research: Theoretical Insights from the work of Pierre Bourdieu', *Penn GSE Perspectives on Urban Education*, 2 (1): 1–25.

Howard, A. (2006) 'Breaking the silence: Power, conflict and contested frames within an affluent high school', *Anthropology and Education Quarterly*, 37 (4): 347–365.

Howard, A. (2009) *Late to class: Social class and schooling in the new economy*. Albany: State University of New York Press.

Howard, A., Wheeler, B. and Polimeno, A. (2014) *Negotiating privilege and identity in educational contexts*. New York: Routledge.

Hurtado, A. (1996) *The color of privilege*. Ann Arbor: University of Michigan Press.

IFS (Institute for Fiscal Studies). (2020) *The impact of undergraduate degrees on lifetime earnings*. London: Department for Education.

Ignatiev, N. (1995) *How the Irish became white*. New York: Routledge.

Inglis, D. (2012) 'Alternative histories of cosmopolitanism', in Delanty, G. (ed.) *Routledge handbook of cosmopolitanism studies*. Abingdon: Routledge.

Jack, A. (2014) 'Culture shock revisited: The social and cultural contingencies to class marginality', *Sociological Forum*, 29 (2): 453–475.

Jack, A. (2016) '"(No) harm in asking": Class, acquired cultural capital, and academic engagement at an Elite university', *Sociology of Education*, 89 (1): 1–19.

Jack, A. (2019) *The privileged poor: How elite colleges are failing the disadvantaged*. Cambridge, MA: Harvard University Press.

Jahi, J. (2014) *Why Isn't My Professor Black?*, https://blogs.ucl.ac.uk/events/2014/03/21/whyisntmyprofessorblack/ (Accessed: 01.11.21).

Karabel, J. (2005) *The Chosen: The hidden history of admission and exclusion at Harvard, Yale and Princeton*. Boston, MA: Houghton, Mifflin.

Keith, M. (2006) *After the cosmopolitan?* London: Routledge.

Kennedy, M. and Power, M. (2008) 'The smokescreen of meritocracy: Elite education in Ireland and the reproduction of class privilege', *Journal for Critical Education Policy Studies*, 8 (2): 223–248.

Kenway, J. and Fahey, J. (2014) 'Staying ahead of the game: The globalising practices of elite schools', *Globalisation, Societies and Education*, 12 (2): 177–195.

Kenway, J., Fahey, J., Epstein, D., Koh, A., McCarthy, C. and Rizvi, F. (2017) *Class choreographies: Elite schools and globalization*. London: Springer.

Kenway, J., Fahey, J. and Koh, A. (2013) 'The libidinal economy of the globalising school market', in Maxwell, C. and Aggelton, P. (eds.) *Privilege, agency and affect: Understanding the production and effects of action*. Hampshire: Palgrave Macmillan, pp. 15–31.

Kenway, J. and Koh, A. (2013) 'The elite schools as 'cognitive machine' and 'social paradise': Developing transnational capitals for the National 'field of power', *Journal of Sociology*, 49 (2–3): 272–290.

Kenway, J., Langmead, D. and Epstein, D. (2015) 'Globalizing femininity in elite schools for girls: Some paradoxical failures of success', in van Zanten, A., Ball, S. and Darchy-Koechlin, B. (eds.) *Elites, privilege and excellence: The national and global Redefinition of educational advantage*. London: Routledge.

Kenway, J. and McCarthy, C. (eds.) (2014) 'Elite schools in globalising circumstances: New conceptual directions and connections', *Globalisation, Societies and Education Special Issue*, 12 (2): 177–195.

Khan, S. (2011) *Privilege: The making of an adolescent elite at St. Pauls school*. Princeton, NJ: Princeton University Press.

Khan, S. (2012) 'The sociology of elites', *Annual Review of Sociology*, 38: 361–377.

Khan, S. (2016) 'The education of elites in the United States', *L'Année sociologique*, 66 (1): 171–192.

Kidder, L. (1997) 'Colonial remnants: Assumptions of privilege', in Fine, M. Weis, L., Powell, L. and Wong, L. (eds.) *Off white*. New York: Routledge, pp. 158–166.

Kincheloe, J. and Steinberg, S. (1998) 'Addressing the crisis of whiteness: Reconfiguring White identity in a pedagogy of whiteness', in Kincheloe, J., Steinberg, S., Rodriguez, N. and Chennault, R. (eds.) *White reign*. New York: St Martin's Griffin, pp. 3–29.

King, N. (2004) 'Using templates in the thematic analysis of text', in Cassell, C. and Symon, G. (eds.) *Essential guide to qualitative methods in organizational research*. London, UK: Sage, pp. 257–270.

Koh, A. (2014) 'Doing class analysis in Singapore's elite education: Unravelling the smoke-screen of 'meritocratic talk', *Globalisation, Societies and Education*, 12 (2): 196–210.

Koh, A. and Kenway, J. (2012) 'Cultivating national leaders in an elite school: Deploying the transnational in the national interest', *International Studies in Sociology of Education*, 22 (4): 333–351.

Kornberger, M. (2015) 'Think different: On studying the brand as organising device', *International Studies of Management and Organisation*, 45 (2): 105–113.

Kynaston, D. and Green, F. (2019) *Engines of privilege: Britain's private school problem*. London: Bloomsbury Publishing Plc.

Kynch, J. and Sen, A. (1983) 'Indian women: Well-being and survival', *Cambridge Journal of Economics*, 7 (3–4): 363–380.

Ladson-Billings, G. (1998) 'Just what is Critical Race Theory and what's it doing in a nice field like Education'? *International Journal of Qualitative Studies in Education*, 11 (1): 7–24.

Ladson-Billings, G. and Tate, W. (1995) 'Toward a critical race theory of education', *Teachers College Record*, 97 (1): 47–68.

Lamont, M. (1992) *Money, morals and manners: The culture of the French and the American upper middle class*. Chicago: University of Chicago Press.

Lamont, M. and Lareau, A. (1988) 'Cultural capital: Allusions, gaps and glissandos in recent theoretical developments', *Sociological Theory*, 6: 153–168.

Lamont, M., Beljean, S. and Clair, M. (2014) 'What is missing? Cultural processes and casual pathways to inequality', *Socio-Economic Review*, 12 (3): 573–608.

Lareau, A. (2003) *Unequal childhoods: Class, race and family life*. Berkeley: University of California Press.

Latour, B. (1999) *Pandora's hope: Essays on the realities of science studies*. Cambridge, MA: Harvard University Press.

Lemann, N. (1999) 'The kids in the conference room', *New Yorker*, October 18: 209–216.

Leonardo, Z. (2002) 'The souls of white folk: Critical pedagogy, whiteness studies, and globalization discourse', *Race Ethnicity and Education*, 5 (1): 29–50.

Leonardo, Z. (2009) *Race, whiteness and education*. New York: Routledge.

Lin, N. (1999) 'Social networks and status attainment', *Annual Review of Sociology*, 25: 467–487.

Lorelli S., Norris, J., White, D. and Moules, N. (2017) 'Thematic analysis: Striving to meet the trustworthiness criteria', *International Journal of Qualitative Research Methodology*, 16: 1–13.

Lowe, R. (2020) 'The Charitable status of elite schools: The origins of a national scandal', *History of Education*, 49 (1): 4–17.

Loyal, S. (2009) 'The French in Algeria, Algerians in France: Bourdieu, colonialism and migration', *The Sociological Review*, 57 (3): 406–427.

Lury, C. (2004) *Brands: The logos of the global economy*. London: Routledge.

Lyotard, J. (1984) *The postmodern condition: A report on knowledge*. Manchester: Manchester University Press.

Marginson, S. (2007) 'The new higher education landscape: Public and private goods, in global/national/local settings', in Marginson, S. (ed.) *Prospects of higher education*. Rotterdam: Brill Sense, pp. 29–77.

Marginson, S. (2008) 'Global field and global imagining: Bourdieu and worldwide higher education', *British Journal of Sociology of Education*, 29 (3): 303–315.

Macfarlane, B. (2015) 'Student performativity in higher education: Converting learning as a private space into a public performance', *Higher Education Research & Development*, 34 (2): 338–350.

Mauss, M. [1925] (1966) *The gift: Forms of function and exchange in archaic societies*. London: Cohen and West.

Maxwell, C. and Aggleton, P. (2013) 'Becoming accomplished: Concerted cultivation among privately educated young women', *Pedagogy, Culture and Society*, 23 (1): 75–93.

McCarthy, C. and Kenway, J. (2014) 'Introduction: Understanding the re-articulations of privilege over time and space', in special issue Elite schools in Globalising Circumstances, *Globalisation, Societies and Education*, 12 (2): 165–176.

McInerney, L. (2013) 'Gove's 'progressive betrayal' seems to be a private school phenomenon', *The Guardian* 17 December. www.theguardian.com/education/2013/dec/17/gove-progressive-betrayal-private-schools (Accessed 30.12.21).

McIntosh, P. (1989) White privilege: Unpacking the invisible knapsack. http://national-seedproject.org/white-privilegeunpacking-the-invisible-knapsack.

McIntosh, P. (1992) 'White privilege and male privilege: A personal account of coming to see correspondences through work in women's studies', in Andersen, M. and Collins, P. (eds.) *Race, Class and gender: An anthology*. Belmont, CA: Wadsworth Publishing, pp. 70–81.

McKinney, K. (2004) *Being white: Stories of race and racism*. New York: Routledge.

Mettler, S. (2014) *Degrees of inequality: How the politics of higher education sabotaged the American dream*. New York: Basic Books.

Miller, J. (2017) *Stain removal: Ethics and race*. Oxford: Oxford University Press.

Morris, D. (2018) 'Are university admissions racially biased?', *Wonkhe*. https://wonkhe.com/blogs/are-university-admissions-racially-biased/.

Moor, L. (2007) *The rise of brands*. Oxford: Berg.

Moore, K. and Reid, S. (2008) 'The birth of brand: 4000 years of branding', *Business History*, 50 (4): 419–432.

Mullen, A. L. (2009) 'Elite destinations: Pathways to attending an Ivy League university', *British Journal of Sociology of Education*, 30 (1): 15–27.

Murphy, J. (1990) *Brand strategy*. Cambridge: Institute of Directors.

Murphy, J. (1998) 'What is branding?' in Hart, S. and Murphy, J. (eds.) *Brands*. Basingstoke: MacMillan, pp. 1–12.

Myers, M. (2022) 'Racism, zero-hours contracts and precarity in UK Higher Education', *British Journal of Sociology of Education*, 43 (4): 584–602.

Myers, M. and Bhopal, K. (2021) 'Cosmopolitan Brands: Graduate students navigating the social space of elite global universities', *British Journal of Sociology of Education*, 42 (5–6): 701–716.

NACUBO. (2020) U.S. and Canadian Institutions Listed by Fiscal Year (FY) 2020 Endowment Market Value and Change in Endowment Market Value from FY19 to FY20. www.nacubo.org/Research/2020/Public-NTSE-Tables (Accessed: 17.03.21).

Ndaji F., Little, J. and Coe, R. (2016) *A comparison of academic achievement in independent and state schools*. Durham, NC: Durham University.

Newman J. (1889) 'The idea of a university defined and illustrated in nine discourses delivered to the Catholics of Dublin', in Ker, I. (ed.) *The idea of a university*. Oxford: The Clarendon Press.

NikeLab. (2021) 'The NSRL Series', www.nike.com/gb/nikelab.

OED. (2017) *New words list June 2017*. https://public.oed.com/updates/new-words-list-june-2017/ (Accessed: 01.11.21).

Omni, M. and Winant, H. (1994) *Racial formation in the United States*. New York: Routledge.

Ostrove, J. and Long, S. (2007) 'Social class and belonging: Implications for college adjustment', *The Review of Higher Education*, 30 (4): 345–363.

Owens, J. and Rivera, L. (2014) '*Recasting the value of an elite education: Institutional prestige, job satisfaction and turnover*', in Paper presented at the Academy of Management annual meeting, Boston, August.

Pásztor, A. and Wakeling, P. (2018) 'All PhDs are equal but. . . Institutional and social stratification in access to the doctorate', *British Journal of Sociology of Education*, 39 (7): 982–997.

Perez, H. and Solorzano, D. (2015) 'Racial macroaggressions as a tool for critical race research', *Race, Ethnicity and Education*, 18: 298–320.

Pilkington, A. (2011) '*Business as usual': Racial inequality in the Academy ten years after Macpherson*. Atlantic Crossings: International Dialogues on Critical Race Theory, 93–114.

Pilkington, A. (2012) 'The internal dynamics of institutional racism in higher education', *Race, Ethnicity and Education*, 16 (2): 225–245.

Preston, J. (2007) *Whiteness and class in education*. The Netherlands: Springer.

Quinn, B. (2018) 'Cambridge University's poor diversity record highlighted by report', *The Guardian* 3 June. www.theguardian.com/education/2018/jun/03/cambridge-colleges-poor-record-on-diversity-highlighted-by-report.

Roediger, D. (1991) *The wages of whiteness*. New York: Verso.

Roediger, D. (2002) *Colored white: Transcending the racial past*. Berkeley: University of California Press.

Rosiek, J. (2019) 'School segregation: A realist's view', *Phi Delta Kappan*, 100 (5): 8–13.

Reay, D. (2017) *Miseducation*. Bristol: Policy Press.

Reeves, A., Friedman, S., Rahal, C. and Flemmen, M. (2017) 'The decline and persistence of the old boy: Private schools and elite recruitment 1897 to 2016', *American Sociological Review*, 82 (6): 1139–1166.

Rehman, R. (2019) 'Universities are still leaving BAME students behind – and the problem goes beyond Oxbridge', *The Independent*, 24 March. www.independent.co.uk/voices/universities-bame-students-inequality-oxbridge-race-a8837771.html.

Rifkind, H. (2019) 'Review: Engines of Privilege: Britain's Private School Problem by Francis Green and David Kynaston – unjust, elitist; please let my kids in; This powerful attack on public schools ends up an unintended advert for them, says Hugo Rifkind', *The Times*, Weekend 1 February.

Rivera, L. (2015) *Pedigree: How elite students get elite jobs*. Princeton University Press.

Robinson, W. (2004) *A theory of global capitalism: Production, class and state in a transnational world*. Baltimore, MD: Johns Hopkins University Press.

Rüegg, W. (eds.) (2003) *A history of the university in Europe*. Cambridge University Press.

Sennett, R. and Cobb, J. (1972) *The hidden injuries of class*. Cambridge: Cambridge University Press.

Simmel, G. (1978) *The philosophy of money*. London: Routledge. (Original work published 1900).

Sklair, L. (2000) *The transnational capitalist class*. Hoboken, NJ: Wiley Blackwell.

Sleeter, C. (1996) 'White silence, white solidarity', in Ignatiev, N. and Garvey, J. (eds.) *Race traitor*. New York: Routledge, pp. 257–265.

Stephens, N., Hamedani, G. and Destin, M. (2014) 'Closing the Social-class Achievement Gap A difference-education intervention improves first-generation students' Academic performance and all students' college transition', *Psychological Science*, 25 (4): 943–53.

Stephens, N., Townsend, S., Markus, H. and Philips, T. (2012) 'A cultural mismatch: Independent cultural norms produce greater increases in cortisol and more negative emotions in first generation college students', *Journal of Experimental Social Psychology*, 48 (6): 1389–1393.

Stevens, M. (2007) *Creating a class: College elites and the making of class*. Cambridge, MA: Harvard University Press.

Stevens, M. L., Armstrong, E. A. and Arum, R. (2008) 'Sieve, incubator, temple, hub: Empirical and theoretical advances in the sociology of higher education', *Annual Review of Sociology*, 34 (1): 127–151.

Stiglitz, J. (1999) 'Knowledge as a global public good', *Global Public Goods*, 1 (9): 308–326.

Stone, L. and Stone, J. (1984) *An open elite: England, 1540–1880*. Oxford: Clarendon Press; New York: Oxford University Press.

Strand, M. and Lizardo, O. (2017) 'The hysteresis effect: Theorizing mismatch in action', *Journal for the Theory of Social Behaviour*, 47 (2): 164–194.

Stuber, J. (2012) *Inside the college gates: How class and culture matter in higher education*. New York: Lexington.

Sutton Trust. (2011) *Degrees of success university chances by individual school*. London: Sutton Trust.

Sutton Trust. (2019) *Sutton trust cabinet analysis* 26 July 2019. www.suttontrust.com/our-research/sutton-trust-cabinet-analysis-2019/.

Sutton Trust/Social Mobility Commission. (2019) *Elitist Britain*. London: Sutton Trust/Social Mobility Commission.

Tamborini, C., Kim, C. and Sakamoto, A. (2015) 'Education and lifetime earnings in the United States', *Demography*, 52 (4): 1383–1407.

Tate, W. F. (1997) 'Critical race theory and education: History, theory, and implications', *Review of Research in Education*, 22: 195–247.

Taylor, E. (2009) 'Introduction', in: Taylor, E., Gillborn, D. and Ladson-Billings, G. (eds.) *Foundations of critical race theory in education*. New York: Routledge.

Thomson, P. (2014) 'Field', in Grenfell, M. J. (ed.) *Pierre Bourdieu: Key concepts*. London: Routledge.

Torres, K. (2009) 'Culture shock: Black students account for their distinctiveness at an elite college', *Ethnic and Racial Studies*, 32 (5): 883–905.

Torres, K. and Charles, C. (2004) 'Metastereotypes and the Black-White Divide: A qualitative view of race on an elite college campus', *Du Bois Review*, 1 (1): 115–149.

Trounstine, J. (2020) 'The geography of inequality: How land use regulation produces segregation', *American Political Science Review*, 114 (2): 443–455.

Turner, C., Clark, A. and Rowan, C. (2021) 'Takes 22 pupils from single elite school', *The Daily Telegraph* Wednesday 16 June. www.telegraph.co.uk/news/2021/06/17/revealed-link-westminster-school-cambridge/ (Accessed: 03.08.21).

UUK/NUS. (2019) *Black, Asian and minority ethnic student attainment at UK universities: Closing the gap*. London: UUK/NUS.

Vaccaro, A. (2014) Harvard's endowment is bigger than half the world's economies. Boston. com www.boston.com/news/business/2014/09/25/harvards-endowment-is-bigger-than-half-the-worlds-economies (Accessed: 12.04.21).

van Eekelen, B. (2015) 'Accounting for ideas: Bringing a knowledge economy into the picture', *Economy and Society*, 44 (3): 445–479.

Van Meter, K. (1990) 'Methodological and design issues: Techniques for assessing the representatives of snowball samples', in Lambert, E. Y. (ed.) *NIDA research monograph 98, from collection and interpretation of data from hidden populations*. Rockville: National Institute on Drug Abuse, pp. 31–43.

Van Zanten, A. and Maxwell, C. (2015) 'Elite education and the state in France: Durable ties and new challenges', *British Journal of Sociology of Education*, 36 (1): 71–94.

Vasagar, J. (2010) 'Twenty-one Oxbridge colleges took no black students last year', *The Guardian* 6 December. www.theguardian.com/education/2010/dec/06/oxford-colleges-no-black-students.

Verger, A., Lubienski, C. and Steiner-Khamsi, G. (2016) 'The emergence and structuring of the global education industry: Towards an analytical framework', in *World yearbook of education*. New York: Routledge, pp. 3–24.

Wacquant, L. (1989) 'Towards a reflexive sociology: A workshop with Pierre Bourdieu', *Sociological Theory*, 7 (1): 26–63.

Wagner, A. (1998) *The new elites of globalisation: Wealthy immigrants in Paris*. Paris: PUF.

Walford, G. (2006) *Private education: Tradition and diversity*. London: Continuum

Walker, P. (2013) 'Michael Gove reveals the surprising inspirations behind his reforms', *The Guardian* 5 February 13. www.theguardian.com/education/2013/feb/05/michael-gove-inspirations-jade-goody (Accessed: 30.12.21).

Warikoo, N. (2016) *The diversity bargain: And other dilemmas of race, admissions and meritocracy at elite universities*. Chicago: University of Chicago Press.

Warikoo, N. (2022) *Race at the top: Asian Americans and whites in pursuit of the American dream in suburban schools*. Chicago: University of Chicago Press.

Warmington, P. (2014) *Black British intellectuals and education: Multiculturalism's hidden history*. London and New York: Routledge.

Warmington, P. (2020) 'Critical race theory in England: Impact and opposition', *Identities*, 27 (1): 20–37.

Warren, J. (2001) 'Doing whiteness: On the performative dimensions of race in the classroom', *Communication Education*, 50 (2): 91–108.

Waters, J. and Brooks, R. (2015) 'The magic operations of separation: English Elite schools on-line geographies, internationalisation and functional isolation', *Geoforum*, 58: 86–94.

Weale, S. (2020) 'BAME students make up one fifth of new Oxford undergraduates', *The Guardian* www.theguardian.com/education/2020/jun/23/bame-students-make-up-one-fifth-of-new-oxford-undergraduates.

Weber, M. (1968) *Economy and society*. New York: Bedminster Press.

Weedon, K. and Grusky, B. (2005) 'The case for a new class map', *American Journal of Sociology*, 111 (1): 141–212.

Weis, L. and Cipollone, C. (2013) 'Class work': Producing privilege and social mobility in elite US secondary schools', *British Journal of Sociology of Education*, 34 (5–6): 701–722.

Weis, L., Cipollone, K. and Jenkins, H. (2014) *Class warfare: Class, race and college admissions in top tier secondary schools*. Chicago: University of Chicago Press.

White, N. (2021) 'Dr Kehinde Andrews: UK's first Black studies professor says his own university is institutionally racist', *The Independent*, 12 June. www.independent.co.uk/news/uk/home-news/kehinde-andrews-birmingham-city-university-b1857395.html (Accessed: 01.01.21).

Williams, J. (2016) 'What so many people don't get about the US working class', *Harvard Business Review*, 10 (2016): 41–47.

Willie, S. (2003) *Acting black: College, identity and the performance of race*. New York: Routledge.

Windle, J. and Nogueira, M. (2015) 'The role of internationalisation in the schooling of Brazilian Elites: Distinctions between two class factions', *British Journal of Sociology of Education*, 36 (1): 174–192.

Wolff, S. (2004) 'Ways into the field and their variants', in Flick, U., von Kardoff, E. and Steinke, I. (eds.) *A companion to qualitative research*. London: Sage, pp. 195–202.

Ye, R. and Nylander, E. (2015) 'The transnational track: State sponsorship and Singapore's Oxbridge elite', *British Journal of Sociology of Education*, 36 (1): 11–33.

Zimdars, A. (2010) 'Fairness and undergraduate admission: A qualitative exploration of admissions choices at the University of Oxford', *Oxford Review of Education*, 36 (3): 307–323.

Zimdars, A., Sullivan, A. and Heath, A. (2009) 'Elite higher education admissions in the arts and sciences: Is cultural capital the key?' *Sociology*, 43 (4): 648–666.

INDEX